Building Successful Partnerships

A Guide for Developing Parent and Family Involvement Programs

National PTA®

NATIONAL EDUCATIONAL SERVICE
Bloomington, Indiana   2000

Published by the National Educational Service
1252 Loesch Road
Bloomington, Indiana 47404-9107
(812) 336-7700
(800) 733-6786
FAX: (812) 336-7790
e-mail: nes@nesonline.com
www.nesonline.com

Cover by Grannan Graphic Design Ltd.
Text design and composition by T.G. Design Group

Printed in the United States of America

Printed on recycled paper

ISBN 1-879639-70-X

DEDICATION

To the founders of the National PTA who recognized, over a century ago, the value and power of parent involvement, and to the millions of PTA members, parents, and educators who continue to meet the profound challenge of creating a better world for children.

CONTENTS

FOREWORD

In 1968 our Yale Child Study Center School Development Program began to encourage meaningful parent partnerships in the two elementary schools in New Haven, Connecticut. More than once we were told, "The parents should raise them, and we will teach them." Some public officials, some behavioral science colleagues, and even some parents agreed that the parents' place was outside the school. Over the years the research has shown that the parents as partners make a positive difference in student school performance. There is a growing consensus that parents and schools should be partners. But there is still significant resistance.

The separation of parent and school is based on a mechanical model of teaching and learning, wrong and outmoded, but still very much alive. In this model, the capacity to learn is thought to be based almost entirely on a child's genetically determined intelligence and will and the teacher's ability and knowledge base. It ignores child development, staff development, and the need to organize and manage schools in a way that nourishes and promotes child development and learning.

It is in such a school that students can attach and bond to staff, as was previously done with parents and caretakers. This promotes identification, initiation, and internalization of the attitudes, values, and ways of the school staff, including the importance of learning and constructive participation in the program of the school. This enables parents and school staff to help young people grow along important development pathways—physical, social interactive, pyscho-emotional, ethical, linguistic, and cognitive. Students who experience such development growth have the best chance to succeed in school and in life.

Underdeveloped or differently developed children are more likely to have school difficulties and drop out. Our country got away with a teaching and learning model that was ineffective for far too many children as long as most who dropped out could work and earn a living without an education, take care of themselves and their families, and become responsible citizens. Family, friend, religious, and other organizations in which families felt belonging—their community—provided children with the motivation to behave in desirable ways. Limited communication and transportation made the meaningful authority figures in the community the carriers of most of the information that children received about the way the world worked. Under these conditions, many adults could censor information until children were able to manage it appropriately, or censure them for acting on it inappropriately. In a sense, the entire community helped parents help children grow up.

At the turn of the century, our country was at a horse and buggy level of technology. In 80 years, it raced through the automobile, airplane, jet, and inter-planetary rocket levels of technology. Because of the related complexity of these advances, children need a higher level of development and education than in the past. But the last half century is the time in the history of the world that information has gone directly to children. It is the first time that children are not growing up in close proximity to their parents and people in their primary social network. And high mobility has decreased the numbers of relatives, friends, and concerned adults in the lives of children. Thus, while children need more help than ever before in handling the usual inner stimulation related to growth and the increased external stimulation, they have less adult support.

Many schools have not adjusted to these changed conditions. Rapid, dramatic change without the kind of school change needed to help students develop to the necessary level is at the heart of academic underachievement and the mild to severe increase in behavior problems among too many of our students nationwide and across the socio-economic spectrum.

In our work at the Yale Center School Development Program, we recreated the essential elements of community in school. A central aspect of this effort was parent and staff partnership—caring, meaningful adults—interacting on behalf of and with students to promote their development, desirable behavior, and learning. *Building Successful Partnerships: A Guide for Developing Parent and Family Involvement Programs* is a comprehensive discussion of why such partnerships are necessary and how to implement them.

The guide presents useful research findings and best practice information in an interesting and thought-provoking way. At the same time, it is a practical and easy to read "how to." It will be helpful to everyone who is working to help schools adjust to the dramatic changes in our country and help students function well.

It is a timely and important book and will grow in importance. In the next few years, policymakers and the public will realize that there is no quick fix for the challenges facing our schools and then the question will be, "Now what?" Support for student development through parent and school partnerships will be a large part of the answer.

—James P. Comer, M.D.
Maurice Faulk Professor of Child Psychiatry
Child Study Center
Yale University

ACKNOWLEDGMENTS

National PTA wishes to acknowledge and express its appreciation to the dedicated group of National PTA board and staff members who contributed to the publication of *Building Successful Partnerships: A Guide for Developing Parent and Family Involvement Programs*. Special thanks is extended to the more than 40 national education, health, and parent involvement groups that have endorsed or supported the National Standards for Parent/Family Involvement Programs (see Appendix D), as well as the countless PTAs, school districts, boards of education, and state departments of education that have adopted and are implementing the National Standards. National PTA further wishes to acknowledge the invaluable feedback provided by the independent reviewers and the professional guidance and support received from the staff of our publisher, the National Educational Service.

National PTA Building Successful Partnerships Editorial Board

Ginny Markell, M.S., President, 1999–2001

Lois Jean White, President, 1997–1999

Shirley Igo, President-elect, 1999–2001

Linda Hodge, Vice President for Programs, 1999–2001

Judy Mountjoy, M.Ed., Vice President for Programs, 1997–1999

Debbie Smith, Parent Involvement Working Group Facilitator, 1999–2001

Parent/Family Involvement Project Team Members 1997-1999: Cara Lockett (leader); Syvonne Forkin; Linda Hamilton; Betty Jacobs; Gail McAda; Delorse McGill; Paula Pawlowski; Connie Ross, M. Ed.; Michael Schloesser; Debbie Smith; Sandy Traeger; and Emilee Yost

National PTA Building Successful Partnerships Staff

Victoria Duran, M.S.W., L.S.C.W., Project Director

Lorenza DiNatale, M.S., Primary Writer

Antoinette Tuscano, Primary Editor and Contributing Writer

Susan Herzog, Editorial Advisor

Jacqueline McCarthy, Design Director

Rosalee Gentile, M.A., Reviewer

Independent Reviewers

Dudley Flood, Ph.D., Retired School Administrator, North Carolina

Benny Gooden, Ed.D., Superintendent of Schools, Fort Smith, Arkansas

Kenneth W. Greene, Ph.D., Superintendent of Schools, Plainview, Texas

Anne T. Henderson, Education Policy Consultant, Institute for Education and Social Policy

John F. (Jack) Jennings, J.D., Director, Center on Education Policy

Kay Luzier, M.A., Title I Teacher on Assignment, Volusia County Schools, Florida; Education Commission Chair, National PTA, 1997–1999

William E. Milliken, President, Communities in Schools, Inc.

Billie Rollins, Director, Strategic Planning and Communications, Council of Chief State School Officers

Larry Saxton, Office Manager, American Association of Colleges for Teacher Education; Co-President, Alice Deal Junior High School PTA, Washington, DC

Harold P. Seamon, Deputy Executive Director, National School Boards Association

Neela Shiralker, Program Associate for Professional Issues, American Association of Colleges for Teacher Education

Neil Shorthouse, M.A., President, Communities In Schools of Georgia

Sue Switzer, Early Childhood Coordinator, Indiana PTA

Manya Unger, National PTA President, 1987–1989

Kathryn Whitfill, National PTA President, 1993–1995

Bob Witherspoon, Senior Research Associate, RMC Research Corporation

INTRODUCTION

WHEN THE SCHOOL DISTRICTS of Clark County, Washington, became concerned about their students' preparedness to enter the work world, they looked outside their schools for help. By enlisting the aid of the county's parents, businesses, and community leaders, the schools were able to create the Clark County Skills Center—a program that provided their high school students with 13 programs teaching a diverse array of skills. In 1983 only 63% of the district's graduates went on to higher education or successful entry-level employment. Ten years later, a follow-up study showed that 94% of the center's graduates went on to higher education or successful entry-level employment. What would have been impossible without outside help became a thriving and successful program.

This community and the many others you will meet in these pages have developed successful partnerships with parents and families, giving them meaningful opportunities to become involved in the education of their children. These communities have empowered their stakeholders—PTA leaders, parents, community members, educators, and administrators—to make a difference in the lives and education of their young people. Research has shown that these kinds of partnerships often produce positive results for students, parents, teachers, and overall school quality.

Building Successful Partnerships: A Guide for Developing Parent and Family Involvement Programs was developed to help you create and foster this same level of involvement in your own community. The need for this book may best be summed up in the motto of the Even Start Program at Cane Run School in Louisville, Kentucky, which is paraphrased from the sayings of Confucius:

Tell me, I'll forget.

Show me, I may remember.

But involve me, and I'll understand.

Building Successful Partnerships was created to help local PTA leaders, principals, teachers, and parent involvement professionals in the crucial work of "involving." It is designed to be a comprehensive and relevant tool for facilitating meaningful discussion among parents, administrators, teachers, parent involvement professionals, Title I coordinators, and leaders of PTAs or other parent groups. By helping these dedicated groups and individuals engage in discussions and planning activities, this book will serve as a foundation for the development of quality parent involvement programs.

The Importance of Parents

We cannot look at the school and the home as being isolated from one another. We must see how the school, community, and the home are interconnected with each other and with the world at large. Successful parent involvement programs will share several fundamental beliefs about parents:

- Parents want what is best for their children.

- Parents, regardless of their background or circumstances, can be a key resource in their children's education.

- All children can learn, and the focus of educators' efforts needs to be on children's success.

- Together, educators, families, and communities can succeed in educating children and preparing them to lead healthy, happy, and productive lives.

To reflect and embrace these beliefs, educators need to recognize that parents must be involved in all aspects of their children's education. It is not enough for them to be involved only at home; they must be involved at all levels in the school—including its governance and decision making.

Henderson and Berla (1995) have noted that the "best results are gained when parents are involved in both learning and decision making" (p. 16). Effectively involving parents requires understanding the four key roles they play in comprehensive and inclusive parent involvement programs. These roles have been adapted from the research of Henderson and Berla (1995) and Lueder (1998).

TEACHERS/NURTURERS—This role focuses on parents' involvement with children's physical, moral, intellectual, emotional, and social development. Parents can nurture this development by providing an appropriate environment that promotes learning and develops the skills and values needed to become physically, psychologically, and emotionally healthy adults.

COMMUNICATORS/ADVISORS—Establishing effective two-way communication between the home and school is this role's focus. In addition, parents must maintain open communication with their children in order to counsel them on personal and educational issues.

SUPPORTERS/LEARNERS—This role focuses on parents obtaining skills and knowledge that will assist them with their children's educational and social development. In turn, parents can contribute their knowledge and skills to the school by enriching the curriculum and providing services and support to students and teachers.

COLLABORATORS/DECISION MAKERS—In this role, parents participate with school staff and educators to help solve problems, make decisions, and develop policies that make the school system more responsive and equitable to all families.

The National Standards for Parent/Family Involvement Programs

The National PTA has long supported the need for effectively involving parents and families in their children's education. In 1997 the National PTA created and adopted the National Standards for Parent/Family Involvement Programs (National PTA, 1998a) to be used along with other education content and performance standards and reform initiatives in support of establishing quality parent involvement programs that influence children's learning and success. Each standard addresses a different type of parent involvement:

- **COMMUNICATING**—Communication between home and school is regular, two-way, and meaningful.

- **PARENTING**—Parenting skills are promoted and supported.

- **STUDENT LEARNING**—Parents play an integral role in assisting student learning.

- **VOLUNTEERING**—Parents are welcome in the school, and their support and assistance are sought.

- **SCHOOL DECISION MAKING AND ADVOCACY**—Parents are full partners in the decisions that affect children and families.

- **COLLABORATING WITH THE COMMUNITY**—Community resources are used to strengthen schools, families, and student learning.

These standards were developed with education and parent involvement professionals through the National Coalition for Parent Involvement in Education (NCPIE). The standards were built upon the work of Joyce L. Epstein, Ph.D., of the Center on School, Family, and Community Partnerships at the Johns Hopkins University, who identified six types of parent involvement.

CHAPTER OVERVIEWS

Before the National PTA began developing *Building Successful Partnerships,* several state PTA presidents interviewed PTA leaders, teachers, principals, and parent involvement professionals from across the country about what kinds of information would be useful in a guide to parent involvement. The National PTA Board of Directors and state parent involvement chairs also contributed their feedback. The responses of these dedicated professionals helped form the book's content.

Building Successful Partnerships replaces an earlier publication, *Parent Plus,* which was produced by the National PTA (1995) before it developed the National Standards for Parent/Family Involvement Programs. These six standards have been integrated into *Building Successful Partnerships,* along with field-tested parent involvement ideas that have proven to be effective.

Chapter 1 focuses on reporting *research findings* on parent involvement and highlights pertinent findings on how parent involvement benefits students, parents, teachers, school quality, and program design. The chapter also reports on how *schools' efforts to include parents* affect parent involvement.

Chapters 2–7 each focus on a specific *program standard* for establishing quality parent and family involvement programs. Each of these chapters contains

- A definition of one of the National Standards for Parent/Family Involvement Programs

- A description of the standard's benefits

- Quality tips to ensure effective use of the standard in developing a parent involvement program

- Project ideas for implementing the standard

- A "Best Practices" section that showcases successful school and/or community programs in the standard area

Chapter 8 focuses on important issues to consider when developing parent involvement programs. These include overcoming *barriers to parent involvement* and knowing how to reach out to the *key players* when forming a program.

Chapter 9 examines three important activities for establishing an effective parent involvement program: developing a *parent/family action team* at your school; creating a *parent/family involvement policy*; and developing a comprehensive *parent/family involvement action plan.*

Chapter 10 summarizes the main ideas in *Building Successful Partnerships* and provides information on opportunities to connect with other individuals and organizations that support parent and family involvement programs.

The **Appendixes** offer a position statement on parent and family involvement; sample surveys, forms, and worksheets; and a list of resources.

Throughout *Building Successful Partnerships,* you will find information that can be applied to different populations in many settings. Any type of school or program can implement the ideas discussed in this book, whether or not it has a PTA. Schools that currently have PTAs can use the book as an assessment tool to evaluate their PTAs' effectiveness in involving parents. In schools without PTAs, another type of parent group or a parent involvement professional can work with school staff, teachers, and administrators to discuss the ideas presented in this book and take action.

Establishing a PTA in your school, however, can enhance the process of creating effective parent involvement programs. The National PTA has a long legacy of advocating on behalf of children and meaningful parent involvement in education. A PTA working at the local level has access to a wide variety of resources and support from both its state PTA and the National PTA to assist it in its endeavors. Working with administrators and teachers, a PTA can function as a critical liaison between the school and the home. For more information, see "About the Author: National PTA®" on page 235.

A FEW WORDS ON LIABILITY ISSUES

In considering any activity that involves parents and other volunteers, it is always important to take into account potential legal liability. Our society has, unfortunately, become quite litigious. Parents and others are occasionally the target of complaints or even lawsuits arising from their volunteer activities.

The federal government and many states have enacted volunteer protection statutes, which go a long way toward discouraging unfounded claims and providing defenses to unfair lawsuits. They do not, however, provide complete protection. Using common sense and knowing what you are legally responsible for can help prevent many legal liabilities. For example:

- Make sure that adequate supervision is provided for all activities involving children.

- Always try to have two adults present.

- Avoid activities where a child or adult might be injured, unless all necessary precautions have been taken.

- If activities are taking place on school property, make sure that they are consistent with school policies.

- And most important, make sure that either the school's liability policy or the PTA's liability policy covers the particular activity in question.

If there is any question about whether a particular activity is covered by the insurance policy, a letter or rider can be obtained from the insurance company to confirm coverage. It is important to note, however, that an insurance policy will not prevent you from being sued. An insurance policy, though, can help protect you financially if you are sued.

DEFINING TERMS

Throughout this book, you will find repeated references to certain terms. The following is an explanation of several of these terms.

Parent

Although we have used the word "parent" in this book to refer to those individuals who are involved in their children's education, we recognize that today other adults may also carry the primary responsibility for a child's education and development. Therefore, all references to parent involvement should be construed as including any adults who play an important role in a child's upbringing and well-being.

Parent Involvement

We define "parent involvement" as the participation of parents in every facet of children's education and development from birth to adulthood, recognizing that parents are the primary influence in children's lives. Parent involvement takes many forms, including

- Two-way communicating between parents and schools

- Supporting parents as children's primary educators and integral to their learning

- Encouraging parents to participate in volunteer work

- Sharing responsibility for decision making about children's education, health, and well-being

- Collaborating with community organizations that reflect schools' aspirations for all children

Schools

References to "schools" may be broadly interpreted to include other programs that serve children and families, such as other academic, specialty, or community programs.

PTAs

References to and sections on how PTAs can be instrumental in promoting and establishing parent involvement programs should be broadly interpreted to apply to other types of parent groups or parent involvement professionals.

BUILDING A FOUNDATION FOR SUCCESS

As the nation focuses on education reform and on setting goals and standards for educational excellence, parents must be involved in the process. Parent and family involvement must be aggressively pursued and supported by families, educators, community members, business people, and governmental agency staff who must work together to improve our children's education. The National PTA believes that parent and family involvement is the foundation upon which all other education reform should be based. Numerous research studies and years of experience in the education field have consistently demonstrated that parent and family involvement in education produces meaningful and lasting results. *Building Successful Partnerships: A Guide for Developing Parent and Family Involvement Programs* will help you involve the parents and families in improving your community's schools.

CHAPTER 1

RESEARCH FINDINGS IN PARENT INVOLVEMENT

RESEARCH SHOWS THAT SCHOOLS with well-structured, consistent parent involvement programs are more likely to experience profound benefits for students, parents, teachers, administrators, and overall school quality. This chapter summarizes results from the pertinent research on this topic.

The most comprehensive survey of research on parent involvement is a series of publications developed by Anne Henderson and Nancy Berla: *The Evidence Grows* (1981); *The Evidence Continues to Grow* (Henderson, 1987); and *A New Generation of Evidence: The Family Is Critical to Student Achievement* (Henderson & Berla, 1995). Citing more than 85 studies, these books document the comprehensive benefits of parental involvement in children's education. Other studies used to compile the findings below are included in the Bibliography that begins on page 231.

PARENT AND FAMILY INVOLVEMENT AND STUDENT SUCCESS

The most accurate predictors of student achievement in school are not family income or social status, but the extent to which a student's family is able to (1) create a home environment that encourages learning; (2) communicate high, yet reasonable, expectations for the child's achievement and future career; and (3) become involved in the child's education at school and in the community.

Findings on Student Achievement

- When parents are involved, students tend to achieve more, regardless of socioeconomic status, ethnic/racial background, or the parents' education level.

- The more extensive the parent involvement, the higher the student achievement.

- When parents are involved in students' education, those students generally have higher grades and test scores, better attendance, and more consistently completed homework.

- Students whose parents are involved in their lives have higher graduation rates and greater enrollment rates in postsecondary education.

- In programs designed to involve parents in full partnerships, student achievement for disadvantaged children not only improves, but can also reach levels that are standard for middle-class children. Children who are furthest behind are most likely to make the greatest gains.

- If parents do not participate in school events, develop a working relationship with their children's educators, or keep up with what is happening in their children's school, their children are more likely to fall behind in academic performance.

Findings on Student Behavior

- When parents are involved, students usually have better attitudes, are more motivated toward school, and have better self-esteem.

- Students whose parents are involved in their education often show improved behavior and have lower rates of suspension for disciplinary reasons.

- Student behaviors such as alcohol use, violence, and antisocial behavior tend to decrease as parent involvement increases.

- Students whose parents are involved in their education are likely to experience improved communication with both their teachers and family.

- Educators tend to hold higher expectations of students whose parents collaborate with teachers. They also hold higher opinions of those parents.

Findings on Culture and Age

- Children from diverse cultural backgrounds tend to do better when parents and professionals collaborate to bridge the gap between the culture at home and the culture in the learning institution.

- The benefits of involving parents are not confined to the early years; there can be significant gains at all ages and grade levels.

- Junior high and high school students whose parents remain involved usually make better transitions, maintain the quality of their work, and develop more realistic plans for their future. Students whose parents are not involved are more likely to drop out of school.

HOW PARENT AND FAMILY INVOLVEMENT BENEFITS PARENTS

Parents can benefit from an involvement in their children's education not only by an improved relationship with their children, but by a heightened sense of confidence, better decision-making and problem-solving skills, and improved self-esteem. The following benefits are often enjoyed by parents who are involved in their children's education.

Social and Emotional Benefits

- Parents show more sensitivity to their children's social, emotional, and intellectual developmental needs.

- Parents become more accepting of their children.

- Parents become more affectionate, use less punishment, and praise their children more often.

Enhanced Problem-Solving Abilities

- Parents use more complex language with their children, encourage their children to verbalize more, and have more positive communication with their children's teachers.

- Parents reason more with their children, place less emphasis on authority as the grounds for desired behaviors, praise children's initiative more, and encourage more exploratory behaviors.

- Parents are more aware of the causes of their children's distress and more skillful in comforting them.

Personal Rewards

- Parents experience higher self-esteem and feel less restricted by child-rearing and homemaking tasks. They find their children more interesting and enjoyable.

- Parents feel more confident in their decision-making skills.

- Parents more often pursue their own educational development.

- Parents more skillfully use community agencies to meet families' and children's needs.

HOW PARENT AND FAMILY INVOLVEMENT BENEFITS EDUCATORS

Parent involvement can support and motivate teachers and principals, allowing them to do their jobs more effectively and with more enjoyment. When there is a strong parent involvement program in place:

- Teachers and principals are more likely to experience improvements in self-esteem and a higher morale.

- Teachers and principals often feel more respect for their profession.

- Job satisfaction can increase among teachers and principals.

- Consistent parent involvement tends to improve communication and relations between parents, teachers, and administrators.

- Teachers and principals often experience improvements in community support of schools.

HOW PARENT AND FAMILY INVOLVEMENT BENEFITS SCHOOL QUALITY

Much discussion on how to improve the quality of education in America has focused on the family's role. Research overwhelmingly supports the fact that high-quality education cannot be successfully achieved without parents' active involvement. Consider the following:

- Schools with a high degree of parent involvement have more support from families and better reputations in the community.

- School programs that involve parents usually outperform identical programs without parent and family involvement.

- Schools where children are failing often improve dramatically when parents are enabled to become effective partners in their children's education.

- The schools' practices to inform and involve parents are stronger determinants of whether inner-city parents will be involved in their children's education than parent education, family size, marital status, and even student grade level.

Research showing that school practices and policies need to be related to family involvement is now reflected in federal policies such as the Goals 2000 Educate America Act. Goal Eight of the Goals 2000: Educate America Act states, "By the year 2000, every school will

RESEARCH

promote partnerships that will increase parental involvement and participation in promoting the social, emotional, and academic growth of children" (National Education Goals Panel, 1998, p. 6).

Congress added this voluntary goal to encourage and increase parent participation in schools across America. It calls upon schools to adopt policies and practices that actively engage parents and families in partnerships that support the academic work of children at home and share decision making at school. Therefore, it prompts schools to examine how their policies, practices, and program designs affect parent involvement. The following section considers what schools need to do to ensure successful parent involvement practices and programs.

WHAT MAKES A PARENT INVOLVEMENT PROGRAM WORK?

Hallmarks of Effective Programs

- For low-income families, a program offering home visits is the most successful way to involve parents. Research also shows that a program offering video or computer-aided instruction at the school can be effective for low-income parents. Parents with at least two years of college education generally prefer receiving parenting information through newsletters, books, and magazines.

- One of the most significant challenges to conducting an effective program is the lack of instruction on parent and family involvement for educators and administrators in their professional training. Effective programs provide these professionals with training and guidance in parent involvement.

- When parents are treated as partners and given relevant information by people with whom they are comfortable, they put into practice the involvement strategies they already know are effective but have been hesitant to use.

- Student achievement tends to be higher in situations where the relationship between parents and educators is a comprehensive, well-planned partnership.

- Collaboration with families is an essential component of a reform strategy, but it is not a substitute for high-quality education programs or comprehensive school improvement.

- When parents receive frequent and effective communication from the school or program, their involvement often increases, their overall evaluation of educators often improves, and their attitudes toward the program are often more positive.

- Parents are much more likely to become involved when educators encourage and assist them in helping their children with their schoolwork.

- Effective programs are usually led by a team of administrators, educators, and parents and usually have access to financial resources.

- When schools create a sense of family and inclusiveness by valuing parents, parents from different cultural backgrounds are more likely to become involved in their children's education.

Teachers, Administrators, and School Staff's Efforts to Involve Parents

Given the last three findings listed above, further discussion is needed on what the research says about educators' effectiveness in involving parents. Studies show that educators often do very well at the following:

- Communicating with parents about their child's progress

- Providing information to parents about their child's development and how it relates to class placement

- Making parents aware of volunteer opportunities at school

(Chandler & Vaden-Kiernan, 1996; Epstein & Dauber, 1991; Epstein & Lee, 1995; National Center for Education Statistics, 1998)

Perhaps one of the most striking examples of involving parents in all aspects of school life can be found in the Comer School Development Program, which was developed by James Comer, Ph.D., and his colleagues at the Yale Child Study Center. This 15-year collaboration with two formerly low-achieving, inner-city New Haven schools has been quite impressive. Dr. Comer's program involves parents in a mental health team, parents' group, and governance and management team that develops a comprehensive school plan that includes academics, social events, and special programs.

On these teams, the principals, parents, teachers, and counselors work together. After 15 years, the New Haven schools have some of the best attendance records in the city, rank among the city's top five in academic performance, and have reported no serious behavior problems at school for more than a decade. The program has been so successful that the Rockefeller Foundation recently dedicated $3 million per year for the next five years to facilitate the spread of this model to schools across the country.

Although research shows that both parents and educators agree on the importance of including parents in the educational process, this general agreement all too often breaks down when it comes to actually implementing a parent involvement program. While parents may want to volunteer for positions that range from classroom assistant to decision maker, many educators still tend to encourage only the more traditional volunteer roles, such as fund-raisers or audience participants at school functions.

Findings vary as to how well educators do in the following areas:

- Providing information to parents on how to help children learn at home and how to help them with homework

- Providing information on community services available to help families

- Providing workshops and classes on parenting skills

- Providing opportunities for parents to be actively involved at the decision-making level in their children's schools

(Chandler & Vaden-Kiernan, 1996; Henderson & Berla, 1995; National Center for Education Statistics, 1998)

Involvement in Developing Education Standards and Student Assessment

Because an increasing number of states are developing education standards and involving parents in the process, it is important for parents to recognize the two different types of standards. Content standards state what students should know and be able to do. Performance standards describe levels of competence or proficiency in specific academic areas. National PTA supports national education standards and believes that through consensus they should be used at the state and local levels among educators, administrators, and parents.

Parents should understand and be involved in the design, development, implementation, and evaluation of student assessment and testing programs. For this to happen, educators should provide parents with easy-to-understand information on the process, along with guidance on how student learning can be increased and on the role parents could play in the process. Research shows that parents who understand the purposes and outcomes of standards-based reforms and are involved in the development and decision-making process are better able to

- Provide at home support of education standards

- Recognize when their children's schools are not improving and hold the schools accountable

- Become better advocates for standards-based reforms

(Lewis & Henderson, 1997)

School Practices and Parent Involvement

Given this information, it is important to look at how school practices are related to actual parent involvement. Studies show that the more effort schools put into informing parents how to be involved in their children's education, the more parent involvement and attendance at school events increase. In schools where parent involvement had been actively sought, parents were most likely to attend events such as parent-teacher conferences, open houses, and back-to-school nights,

RESEARCH

and, to a lesser extent, plays or performances featuring their children. In addition, "school events that featured interaction with a child's teacher appeared to attract the greatest attendance" (Chandler & Vaden-Kiernan, 1996; National Center for Education Statistics, 1998, p. 13).

Two different parent involvement studies, both with positive findings overall, highlighted concerns regarding the limited types of parent involvement that many schools are actively seeking. In the first study, done in 1996 by Chandler, Vaden-Kiernan, and researchers from the National Center for Education Statistics (NCES), approximately 21,000 parents were surveyed. In the second study, done in 1998, NCES researchers surveyed principals, teachers, or other school staff active in parent involvement from 900 public elementary schools.

Factors Affecting Parent Involvement

These studies reveal that many factors influence the amount, type, and quality of parent involvement, and that various differences and similarities emerge from the many different types of schools and communities. Compared to smaller rural schools, larger urban schools with a high number of students living in poverty and a high minority enrollment tend to provide more information on community services, have more parenting skills workshops and classes, and have an advisory council that involves parents. In the 1998 NCES survey mentioned above, one quarter to one third of the schools reported involving parents in decision making to a moderate extent (pp. 1, 16–17). However, schools with advisory councils that included parents were more likely to listen to parents' input than schools without such councils.

In general, schools with high numbers of students living in poverty and high minority enrollments reported less positive parent involvement than schools that were lower in these categories (Epstein, 1995; National Center for Education Statistics, 1998). This information is crucial and suggests that schools with these characteristics may have specific issues that function as barriers to successful parent involvement.

Although there is no magic formula for creating successful parent involvement programs in schools that serve poor children, minority children, or both, research does indicate several important factors. According to research, lower-income parents often become passionately involved in their children's school when that school adopts as part of its mission an inclusive policy that helps families feel valued, encouraged, and supported (Lewis & Henderson, 1997). Furthermore, research indicates that schools are most successful when they collaborate with parents to bridge the gap between the culture at home and in the school by providing helpful information and teaching skills that encourage parents to

- Create learning environments at home

- Have positive attitudes toward education

- Have high expectations of children

Studies show that when these efforts are made, children from all backgrounds tend to do well (Henderson, 1987, p. 8), and schools experience "significant and long-lasting parent involvement regardless of the social, economic, or ethnic background of the parents" (Henderson & Berla, 1995, p. 14).

Research also shows that fathers, single parents, parents who work outside the home, and parents who live far from school are less likely to be involved at their children's school (Brimhall, West, & Winquist-Nord, 1997; Epstein, 1995; U.S. Department of Education, 1997). In addition, research indicates that educators' efforts to involve parents usually decrease as children enter middle school and high school, and that parents are generally less involved in their children's education as their children grow older. These barriers to parent involvement and strategies to overcome them will be examined further in chapter 8.

WHAT SCHOOLS CAN DO

When it comes to parent involvement and its powerful influence, the knowledge base is broad and clear on its positive effects. The challenge, however, comes in transforming knowledge into practice, and practice into results. Studies show that although there is agreement on the importance of parent involvement, and despite educators' good intentions, efforts to meaningfully involve parents can sometimes fall short. The National PTA responded to this challenge by developing the National Standards for Parent/Family Involvement Programs. These standards are research-based and grounded in both sound philosophy and practical experience. The purposes of the program standards are as follows:

- To promote meaningful parent and family participation

- To raise awareness regarding the components of effective programs

- To provide guidelines for schools and communities that wish to improve their programs

There is no one formula for success in creating a "partnership school" that bonds families and educators together in working toward a common goal. The overall integration of practices and characteristics that a school adopts should be based on local needs and circumstances. The National PTA, however, believes that the national program standards provide a basic blueprint for building the most effective and inclusive types of parent involvement programs. They can be used as guidelines to direct leaders of institutions that serve parents and families as they develop meaningful, well-planned, and long-lasting parent involvement programs. They can also be used to evaluate the effectiveness of long-term school reform efforts to actively involve families in their children's education.

The program standards and several of their guiding principles are as follows:

STANDARD I. COMMUNICATING—Communication between home and school is regular, two-way, and meaningful.

- Involve all families, not simply those most easily reached. Pay special attention to parents who work outside of the home, single parents, and parents from different cultures.

- Communicate clearly and frequently with parents about school policies and programs and their children's progress.

STANDARD II. PARENTING—Parenting skills are promoted and supported.

- Provide resources, classes, and workshops to support and strengthen the skills needed by all parents to effectively fulfill their role.

STANDARD III. STUDENT LEARNING—Parents play an integral role in assisting student learning.

- Treat parents as partners in the education process by providing them with the necessary resources and instruction to serve as active participants in their children's learning.

STANDARD IV. VOLUNTEERING—Parents are welcome in the school, and their support and assistance are sought.

- Create a school climate that is open, helpful, and friendly.

STANDARD V. SCHOOL DECISION MAKING AND ADVOCACY—Parents are full partners in the decisions that affect children and families.

- Encourage parents, both formally and informally, to comment on school policies and to share decision-making opportunities.

- The principal and other school administrators should actively express and promote the philosophy of partnership with all families.

STANDARD VI. COLLABORATING WITH THE COMMUNITY—Community resources are used to strengthen schools, families, and student learning.

- Establish partnerships that are mutually beneficial and structured to connect individuals, not just institutions or groups.

> The six program standards should be implemented together so that they have a synergistic effect, each multiplying the effects of the others. Together they are most effective and deliver their most powerful impact.

These six standards are discussed in more detail in the following chapters through quality tips, project ideas, best practices, and other strategies for successfully implementing each standard. The standards can be used as guidelines

- To direct leaders of institutions with programs serving parents and families as they move from discussion toward developing meaningful, well-planned, and long-lasting parent involvement programs

- To evaluate the effectiveness of long-term school reform efforts to actively involve families in their children's education

CHAPTER 2

STANDARD I: COMMUNICATING

Definition: Communication between home and school is regular, two-way, and meaningful.

THIS FIRST STANDARD—COMMUNICATING—is the essential foundation upon which all the other standards are built. It is the cornerstone for building a solid school-family partnership. When parents and educators effectively communicate, students benefit, the potential for conflict is reduced, and life becomes less stressful for administrators and teachers.

Effective home-school communication is the two-way sharing of information vital to student success. This type of effective partnering requires give-and-take conversations, goal setting, and regular follow-up interactions. Some educators are still reluctant to use more effective means of communication, viewing the task as too difficult, too time consuming, or too much work. Too often, such feelings result in one-way communication from the school without the exchange of ideas and perceptions. This chapter will demonstrate how investing in proactive communication requires little or no extra time. In fact, making the investment from the beginning can even save time during the school year, because the more frequently teachers communicate, the more effective they become at it. This results in parents becoming more cooperative and the principal needing to spend less time mediating between angry and frustrated parents and teachers. The end result is a positive learning environment for all children.

RESEARCH FINDINGS

Research has shown that consistent, two-way communication between the home and the school often provides the following benefits (Epstein, Coates, Clark-Salinas, Sanders, & Simon, 1997).

Students

- Gain an awareness of their own progress and competence

- Understand expectations and rules

- Become more aware of their role in the partnership and can serve as information couriers

Parents

- Report a greater belief in their ability to influence their children

- Better understand school programs and policies

- Are aware of their children's progress

- Evaluate their children's teachers as more effective

- Become more involved in their children's learning

Teachers and Administrators

- Appreciate and make more effective use of parent volunteers

- Gain an increased ability to seek and understand family views on children's progress

- Achieve greater teaching effectiveness

COMMUNICATING WITH PARENTS

To establish clear and effective communication, PTA members, educators, and school administrators and staff must first look at their own attitudes about informing parents and at how they communicate with families. Body language, lack of eye contact, and covert conversations can communicate rejection and hostility and can leave parents feeling that efforts to be friendly and open are insincere. Educators and PTA leaders need to concentrate not on what parents know or on what they think parents know, but on what parents can *come* to know. Teacher and author Cindy Christopher believes that educators must let go of the assumption that parents do not want to be involved. In her book, *Building Parent-Teacher Communication: An Educator's Guide* (1996), Christopher states that parents do want to get involved, but "often just do not know how" (p. 13).

PTAs and educators need to support families so that parents can understand and become comfortable with the school system. To do this, school representatives at every level must play a part.

ADMINISTRATORS—Administrators are the keys to establishing a sense of welcome to families and providing friendly access to school buildings. To make parent involvement work, administrators need to provide direction and leadership and model a welcoming attitude toward parents and families.

SUPPORT STAFF—Secretaries, custodians, and security personnel are generally the first people parents meet when they enter their children's school. Support staff members need to welcome parents with their tone of voice, body language, and friendliness.

TEACHERS—Teachers can play a special role in giving parents access to their children's world at school. Teachers need to examine their beliefs about parents' roles, assess how openly and honestly they communicate with families, and determine how welcome parents feel in their classrooms.

PTA LEADERS—PTAs provide many potential opportunities for family involvement at school. To ensure participation in meetings and activities, PTA leaders and officers need to consider how well they communicate to a diverse group of parents and how well the PTA addresses the needs of all families.

COMMUNICATING

It is important to consider written communication as well. To communicate clearly with parents, information should be written in plain language and not in jargon or acronyms. It should also be sensitive in its tone. Some writing styles complicate communication and seem exclusive, confusing parents and sometimes making them angry. Finally, information may need to be translated into other languages, so that all parents can understand what is being sent home. This is especially important when talking to parents about education standards and student assessment and testing.

QUALITY TIPS FOR SUCCESSFUL PROGRAMS

It is one thing to talk about communication and increasing parent involvement. It is, however, quite another thing to take the time and effort necessary to learn how to effectively communicate with each other. The following suggestions are provided to help teachers, administrators, PTA leaders, and parents communicate with each other.

Tips for Parents and Teachers

GIVE POSITIVE FEEDBACK. Acknowledge a teacher's, child's, or parent's positive strengths, talents, achievements, and behaviors, and show appreciation for what he or she has done.

BE ON THE "SAME PAGE." Share your wishes and worries about a child. When this happens, both the teacher and the parent learn what the other has observed about the child's interests and motivations and can help each other provide the child with the best learning environment possible at home and at school. Set expectations and goals together at the beginning of the school year.

SOLVE IT EARLY. Teachers and parents should initiate a conversation with one another before there is a negative issue or crisis. Be open to any information—positive or negative. If you are having difficulty communicating for any reason, respectfully let the other person know why, and try to resolve it together before going to the principal for help.

Tips for PTA Leaders, Administrators, and Teachers

GO WHERE YOU NEED TO BE. Actively recruit parents' support. Communication is better between home and school if parents are active in the school, so reach out to parents and meet them on their turf. Make home visits or hold a meeting at a community center, park building, or meeting room in a temple, church, synagogue, or mosque.

GET TO KNOW EACH OTHER INFORMALLY. Provide and seek out informal opportunities to talk with and get to know parents, administrative staff, and teachers.

SPEAK THE SAME LANGUAGE. Use support staff, other parents, or family advocates as translators at meetings and conferences. Send home all information in the parents' native language. If a parent has difficulty reading, substitute phone calls for written communication.

SHARE INFORMATION. Provide clear information regarding course expectations, student placement, school activities, student services, and optional programs. Disseminate information on school reforms, policies, discipline procedures, assessment tools, and school goals, and include parents, teachers, or administrators in any related decision making. Regularly distribute student work for parental comment and review.

Tips for Everyone

MAKE AN APPOINTMENT. Give teachers, parents, or administrators some advance notice that you would like to meet with them, and let them know what you would like to discuss. Ask them how much contact they want to have and how they prefer to communicate (e-mail, phone, notes, or in person).

LEAVE YOUR BAGGAGE AT THE DOOR. Put previous negative experiences with teachers, parents, or administrators behind you and begin each interaction with an open mind and positive attitude.

SHARE THE SAME GOALS. Agreeing on the following three goals may help teachers, parents, and administrators to improve communication and establish good home-school partnerships:

1. Build each child's self-esteem and encourage children to do their best. Avoid applying unnecessary pressure by setting unrealistic goals. Avoid ridicule or public criticism.

2. Hold high standards. Expect that all children can learn, and help them do so. Treat all children fairly. Do not play favorites.

3. Stress positive discipline and responsibility, and establish clear and fair rules that are regularly enforced and fully explained. Stress that basic school rules and expectations should mirror those at home, so consistency is provided for a child. Reinforce positive behavior.

PTAs AND ADMINISTRATORS WORKING TOGETHER

A Four-Step Plan for Success

PTAs can play an important role by serving as the communication link between school and home. This role includes working with a school's teachers and principal, and sometimes with the school district, to gather information about parents. PTAs also form teams with school staff, teachers, and administrators to educate them on the importance of meaningful, two-way, and consistent communication. These teams increase communication by going into the community and meeting with parents to discuss the school and students. They also make parents feel welcome in the school. The four steps below are suggestions for how PTAs and administrators can work together.

1. Invite a speaker from a local college or counseling center to discuss various communication styles and facilitate a communications workshop for all school staff, administrators, educators, and parents. Consider holding the workshop at a community center or park building to help ensure a good attendance by parents, and require all school staff and educators to participate. Having the initial workshop conducted by someone not directly connected to the school can serve as an icebreaker by putting everyone at ease and establishing a warm and open climate for future discussion.

2. Form a communication team of parents, teachers, and administrators that explores home-school communication in depth. All participants will need to establish and agree that this will be a safe place for open and honest communication, that all perspectives will be welcomed and listened to, and that judgments will be suspended. Decide which communication issues need to be discussed. Come to a consensus on how to share this information with the whole school and how to further involve others in the discussion.

3. Hold in-service sessions on communication for teachers, support staff, and school administrators. Invite parents, and consider holding these sessions at times that are easiest for parents to attend. Workshop topics should emerge from the communication team's discussions, and workshops should be collaboratively developed and facilitated by team members. Strive to actively involve as many participants in as many of the discussions as possible. These strategies help all participants take ownership for the ideas and plans that evolve.

    Topics might include the following:

    *   How parents can speak to teachers

    *   How teachers, support staff, and administrators can speak to parents

    *   How to ask difficult questions without finger-pointing and blaming

    *   How to effectively and inclusively communicate with all parents

    Workshops should also focus on how the school will effectively

    *   Articulate the school's vision, policies, and expectations of parents and students

    *   Share information relating to a child's progress, such as improving report cards and parent-teacher conferences

- Investigate how to establish or improve the school's learning standards and parents' and teachers' understanding of these standards

4. Write down the communication team's ideas on creating goals and plans for putting good communication processes in place among school staff, the principal, educators, and parents. Writing down the ideas provides a record that the team can use to help assess progress as well as validate the team's work. Distribute these ideas to all parents, school staff, teachers, and the principal. Creating action teams and action plans will be discussed in detail in chapter 9.

ADMINISTRATORS, EDUCATORS, AND PARENTS WORKING TOGETHER

Handling Conflict

The strategies in this chapter can help school administrators, educators, and parents avoid conflict with each other. When conflicts occur, the best strategy is to contact the teacher, parent, or principal involved in the conflict right way. Do not let issues fester for a long time. Whether you make contact over the phone or in a face-to-face meeting, planning is the key to a productive encounter. Write down what you plan to say before you call or meet. The following guidelines will help you successfully handle such a meeting:

1. Start with a statement of concern.

2. Describe the specific behaviors or issues that have necessitated the call or meeting.

3. Describe the steps you have taken or have considered taking to solve the problem.

4. Present the part you will play in solving the problem.

5. Express confidence that you can solve the problem together.

6. Plan for a follow-up contact to discuss progress on the situation or behavior.

Making the serious commitment to have two-way and meaningful communication opens the door to honest emotion and sometimes anger. If conflict occurs, and someone becomes angry, it is critical to properly manage the situation, minimize the anger's destructive nature, and return the communication to a positive and creative focus. The following strategies can help you handle an outburst of anger.

EXPRESS CONFIDENCE. Remain calm. Use a steady tone of voice. Listen and try to calm the other person down. Be prepared to "hear them out," and then examine the facts together. Ask questions to clarify issues and feelings. State your facts in the form of questions (this is less threatening and can disarm someone's anger). For example, instead of saying, "Here is the problem as I see it," say, "I would like to ask some questions to get a handle on the problem as I see it. Is that all right?"

ESTABLISH GROUND RULES. Set time limits for the discussion and schedule another one if needed. Rearrange the furniture, if necessary, to remove barriers between you and the other person. Clearly state at the beginning that yelling or profanity should be avoided and that each person should show the other courtesy and respect.

SLOW DOWN THE PACE. Pause and reflect on what is being said. Repeat what someone has said to clarify your understanding. Take notes to show that the person's concerns are important and need to be accurately recorded.

RESPECT THE RIGHT TO DISAGREE. The purpose of these strategies is not to suppress conflict, but to minimize the destructive nature of anger. The end goal is not necessarily to agree, but to respect the views of others and try to transform anger into a creative force by moving the discussion toward a collaborative understanding of the issues as much as possible.

SUCCESSFUL PTA MEETINGS

Planning for better communication begins at PTA meetings. For PTAs to be a successful communication link between the school and the home, PTA meetings need to model supportive and inclusive communication practices. These practices can be applied to any type of parent-led meeting.

Make Meetings Easier for Everyone to Attend

- Hold meetings outside of school at locations such as apartment complex community rooms, community centers, or other central locations, to enable more parents to attend.

- Send invitations by phone or mail.

- Offer materials presented at the meetings in the language or languages that parents can read. If you have only one other major language represented at your school besides English, consider conducting meetings in both languages. This will take more time, but will also make everyone feel equally included.

Make Meetings at School More Inviting

- Form a carpool network to help parents who do not have transportation. If the school administration permits use of a school bus, arrange group pickups and drop-offs in communities where many parents do not have transportation.

- Consider holding both a morning meeting and an evening meeting so that parents can attend the one more convenient for them. Work with other local schools to stagger PTA meeting times for parents with children in different schools.

- Advertise the PTA at school. During the first meeting of the year, explain what a PTA is, introduce the local PTA's officers and lead volunteers, and display materials that explain all child-related programs.

- Offer refreshments or low-cost meals at evening meetings. Provide child care for all meetings, and provide homework assistance in the library for evening meetings.

Make Meetings More Interesting

- Plan agenda topics based on issues important to parents and the current needs of their children. Conduct a survey that asks parents to identify what critical issues they are facing and want to discuss at meetings and what needs must be met for them to attend meetings.

- Schedule dynamic speakers for meetings, then advertise them.

- Use PTA meetings to conduct discussion groups on education topics such as school funding, testing and assessment, legislation and its effects on school programs, and so forth.

- Encourage people to participate in school board meetings.

- Set ground rules for communication and follow them.

- Recognize outstanding students in all areas of school activities.

PROJECT IDEAS

Schoolwide activities play a major role in reinforcing or undermining a school's goals. When planning PTA and schoolwide activities, consider implementing projects in each of the six standards to ensure a comprehensive approach to parent involvement. Activity ideas should stress what is important, be inclusive, foster an appreciation for differences, and help build a sense of community among parents, students, teachers, and administrators. PTA projects should supplement and enhance the projects sponsored by the school and should be planned with teachers and administrators.

Any form of communication needs to be sensitive to the changing nature of the American family. PTA members and educators need to consider the diversity of the parents at their school when sending home important information and planning events. Accommodate cultural diversity by using translators to make phone calls to parents who do not speak English, sending home all mail in the major languages represented at your school, and offering English as a second language (ESL) classes or computer software at the school to help parents interested in learning

COMMUNICATING

English. It is also important to take into consideration single-parent families and children being raised by grandparents, fathers, and young mothers when distributing information and planning events.

PLAN FOR LONG-TERM SUCCESS

When planning projects, remember the lasting effect PTA members and educators want the project to have on improving student achievement, increasing parent involvement, and so forth. Plan projects that can become a standard practice in the school, such as incorporating an event into a school's improvement plan. Ideally, events should be held several times during the school year with activities planned between events. Projects should also be evaluated, improved, and continued each year so that they become ongoing programs (Henderson, Jones, & Raimondo, 1999). Chapter 9 provides further information on creating action plans and evaluating activities.

Ideas for PTAs and the School Community Working Together

Verbal Communication

ASK THE RIGHT QUESTIONS. Recruit volunteers or school staff to conduct interviews or surveys, or sponsor a "question roundup" or "suggestion derby" to help motivate parents to communicate and assess their communication needs. In addition, ask parents what they want to know about the school or their children's education and what is the best way to communicate with them.

GETTING TO KNOW YOU. Throughout the school year, sponsor events and activities in which educators and parents can interact informally and get to know each other better.

Written Communication

BENVENUTO! BIENVENIDOS! WELCOME! Place large signs welcoming visitors at all the school's entrances and on each classroom door. They may be as simple as, "Welcome," or as detailed as, "Welcome, parents and visitors. Please come to the office so that we can help you." These signs should be written in all the major languages spoken in the community.

FOLLOW THE YELLOW BRICK . . . FOOTPRINTS? Post a staff roster with room numbers outside the main office, along with a map of the school to help direct parents. Consider using color-coded lines or footprints on hallway floors so parents can easily find the important places they need to go. For example, they could follow the blue line to the library or the yellow footprints to the parent center.

PARENT HANDBOOK. Work with parents to develop a parent handbook that includes the school's rules and policies as well as the school's mission and goals; information on curriculum, learning standards, assessment procedures and tools; and ways for parents to be actively involved in the school. Promote the handbook to parents by highlighting examples of the book's information in school newsletters and other forms of home-school communication. Hold a special parent night and provide an overview of the contents of the book. Also, post the handbook online on your school's or PTA's web page.

NEWS YOU CAN USE. Appoint a PTA newsletter chairperson to work with the school to help produce or contribute to the school newsletter to make it relevant, useful, and timely for parents. The newsletter should be written in plain, easy-to-understand language. If education terminology must be used in the newsletter, provide definitions. Before printing the final version, have a parent volunteer read a draft and provide feedback. Include a means for two-way communication in each newsletter, such as a question-and-answer section or a mini-survey. Encourage the school to mail the newsletter directly to parents.

MAKING CONTACT: WHEN AND HOW. Publicize the hours when administrators and teachers are available for parent visits along with any procedures for contacting teachers by telephone or in writing. Send home a teacher directory that lists each teacher's name and provides the phone number of the school and/or each teacher's extension, along with the times they are available for contact.

COMMUNICATING

Parent-Teacher Conferences

CONFERENCING THROUGHOUT THE YEAR. Plan three parent-teacher conferences—one at the beginning of the school year, one in the middle, and one at the end—to establish mutual expectations and understand family/child strengths, needs, and progress. Educators should schedule home visits when appropriate.

LETTING STUDENTS LEAD. Investigate how to conduct student-led parent-teacher conferences for middle and high school students. Consider having separate grade-level meetings for the parents of freshmen, sophomores, and so forth.

MAKING THE MOST OF THE CONFERENCE. Send home an invitation to the conference that includes questions and/or ideas for parents to think about. In consultation with educators, develop a publication on preparing for parent-teacher conferences with sample questions for parents to help them work more effectively with teachers. At back-to-school nights, faculty meetings, or both, present role plays that demonstrate to parents and teachers the best ways to share information and plans at parent-teacher conferences.

MARK YOUR CALENDARS. Distribute calendars that contain upcoming school and classroom events, programs, and classroom assignments. Establish dates for when parents should follow up with teachers on students' progress.

Training

EFFECTIVE COMMUNICATION TECHNIQUES. Educate parents, administrators, teachers, and school support staff (including secretaries and custodians) on effective communication techniques.

DIVERSITY TRAINING. Provide diversity training for teachers, school staff, and school administrators on working and communicating with diverse families. Contact the school district's central office or the leaders of local cultural organizations for leads in identifying potential instructors.

Technology

Establish a school web page that contains information about your school, upcoming events and news, and PTA meetings. Also encourage your school district or PTA to create a web page.

LOG ON TO THE NATIONAL PTA. Work with your local library to create a special web page that would make National PTA's website (www.pta.org) and your local school's website available for all parents to access.

GET WIRED TO COMMUNICATE. Advocate before school policymakers for school staff to have adequate access to telephones and other means of communication. If equipment or wiring is a problem, seek funding for a technology upgrade or arrange a cooperative project with a local telephone service provider, school business partner, or technology company. Advocate for the school to develop and implement a technology plan.

SET UP A SCHOOL HOTLINE. Establish a school or district hotline staffed by parent volunteers and translators who can answer parents' questions and provide information. Include a recording on the hotline that provides information on assignments due, suggestions for home learning, classroom activity updates, and homework assistance.

VIDEOS. For parents who have a difficult time coming to school, create and send them short, informative videos about the school's programs and services.

Ideas for Teachers

Before School Begins

GET ORIENTED! To help prepare children for the next grade, work with other teachers of all grade levels in the school to host an orientation night before the school year begins. Introduce yourself to parents, and share your expectations for students regarding homework, discipline, and the materials they will need. Explain what you will cover during the school year and tell them how much you look forward to having parents volunteer in the classroom.

SUMMERTIME ACTIVITIES. Mail home summertime parent/child learning activity calendars. Conduct summertime home visits or make personal phone calls to parents.

During the School Year

KEEP IT CONSTANT, KEEP IT POSITIVE. Make phone calls or send e-mail to contact parents regularly about their children's progress. Try to make three positive contacts for every negative one.

MONTHLY CLASSROOM BULLETINS. Send home an interactive notebook in which parents and teachers can write down questions, comments, or concerns. The student then brings the notebook back to school for the teacher to read. In addition, send a monthly newsletter home with students to keep parents informed about classroom news, highlight their children's positive behavior and achievements, and encourage ongoing communication.

KEEP PARENTS IN THE PLANNING LOOP. On the first day of school, send home a discipline plan to parents that explains classroom rules, consequences for breaking rules, and rewards for good behavior. Include an acknowledgement section at the bottom of the letter that parents can sign and return to school. Use this format for communicating homework plans and other information about your classroom to parents.

"DEAR DIARY . . ." Create a journal for each student. Each day, send the journals home with students so they can read their comments about their school day to their parents. Have parents sign the day's entry before the students bring the journal to school the next day. By the end of the year, this journal will be a great keepsake for students and parents.

Ideas for PTAs Working With Middle and High School Communities

TRANSITION ORIENTATIONS. Provide special orientations for parents whose children are entering middle or high school for the first time. Include administrative presentations that highlight the policies and expectations in the parent handbook, discuss the similarities and differences between the former school environment and the new one, provide a student-guided tour of the facility, serve dinner in the cafeteria, and arrange visits with counselors and teachers.

ADVOCATES. Help keep students in school by encouraging custodians, school secretaries, librarians, and others to get to know particular children well and serve as advocates for those students. Advocates can also become partners with parents, sharing in students' successes and concerns.

SECURITY WITH COURTESY. When parents must go through gates, metal detectors, and check-in procedures to enter the school, ensure that they know that such devices and procedures are in place to protect students, not to keep parents out. Provide security personnel with some customer-service training to create a welcoming climate for parents.

SHARING INFORMATION. Send home classroom newsletters written by students, postcards with positive comments, and daily or weekly attendance/academic check sheets that both parents and teachers can mark to show completion of student assignments and attendance.

TAPPING STUDENT LEADERS. Encourage the school superintendent to work with parents, teachers, and the principal to establish a Parent-Teacher-Student Association (PTSA). Encourage students to serve as co-officers and chairs to bring their ideas to PTA planning sessions. Check state law to determine if a youth under 18 can serve as an officer of an organization.

BEST PRACTICES

A "Best Practices" section is included at the end of each of the six chapters (chapters 2–7) that addresses the National Standards for Parent/Family Involvement Programs. These sections provide examples of how parent groups, educators, and community leaders are currently implementing the national standards in their own schools and communities.

Each community and each set of volunteers are unique. These programs should be considered as guidelines. If you think a program might work for you, adapt it to your situation.

The Future of Communication

The state of Utah's PTA, along with teacher educators, teachers, administrators, and parents, became part of the Utah Office of Education's Center for Families in Education task force. Their mission was to develop a college course to help future teachers learn specific communication skills that would increase parent involvement and student performance—a skill that future teachers were not acquiring in college.

The result of the task force's work was a one-quarter, 10-hour class that included information on parent involvement, communication skills, family structures, home-school relations, and family advocacy and governance. The first class was taught at Utah State University in 1995.

Utah PTA members gave presentations to the class on the benefits of parent involvement in the classroom and the school's responsibilities to both parents and students. PTA members also discussed the information in the *National Standards for Parent/Family Involvement Programs* guide.

The BUDDIES System

Sometimes, all it takes to get involved in your children's education is having a buddy. At Guilford Primary School in Greensboro, North Carolina, the buddies were part of a program called Building Unity Despite Diversity in Every Situation (BUDDIES) that started in the 1997–1998 school year.

With the help of a teacher of English as a second language, PTA members created and sent out a survey in several different languages, asking parents which languages were spoken at home and how well they could read and write English and other languages.

The survey helped identify the language strengths and barriers of the school's families. This information was then used to pair up families for the year based on language ability. For example, a family bilingual in Spanish and English would be paired with another family who spoke

Spanish, but little or no English. The bilingual family would then translate important school information into Spanish for its BUDDIES family.

As part of the program, 1,700 people attended a multicultural night held for families to display and view artifacts and crafts from each other's cultures. This program won the National PTA's 1999 Outstanding Unit for Parent Involvement Award, which was presented as part of an annual and national awards program.

Speak Out

Communication between adolescents and adults became a little bit easier in Eau Claire, Wisconsin, after a series of forums were hosted by the DeLong PTA of the DeLong Middle School. The forums were sponsored by the PTA, the school district, an area youth organization, and the local police department.

At one youth forum, 5 parents and 25 students from three middle schools and two high schools in Eau Claire formed a panel to discuss their identities as students and parents, as well as issues and concerns unique to each group. They also discussed factors that can contribute to misunderstandings between the two groups. Two school staff members facilitated the evening, which included role playing by the teen panel and a question-and-answer segment.

About six to eight people were members of the core planning committee for each forum. Committee members included a local principal, two school board members, PTA officers, a member from a local youth organization, and a representative from the area's local newspaper. Topics that might be discussed at youth forums include sexuality and teen pregnancy, gay and lesbian issues, alcohol and drugs, and creating a family-friendly school.

Life After High School

The fact that not all teens are prepared for life after high school prompted the PTA at Shawnee Mission South High School in Overland Park, Kansas, to conduct a program for high school seniors and their parents called "Life After High School—How Do I Survive?"

COMMUNICATING

With student and staff input, PTA members compiled a list of 12 topics and recruited local experts for a daytime workshop program for students. The topics included financial management, insurance coverage, personal safety inside and outside of dating situations, adjusting to college life, and options beyond a four-year college. Students picked 6 of the 12 topics, and then PTA members assigned students to their workshops, times, and rooms. The program also included a panel of high school alumni who were either in college or on the job who talked about their experiences and answered students' questions.

The day after the students' program, the PTA hosted a different program for the parents with others speakers, including an insurance broker and an attorney who talked about the responsibilities parents have for their 18-year-old children.

Planning for the project included brainstorming for topic areas and presenters, submitting a detailed program plan to the principal for discussion, writing a letter to faculty members requesting their support for the program, arranging for a parent volunteer and a teacher to be in each workshop to assist the speaker, and providing a light meal and a briefing to the presenters and volunteer staff before the program.

Multilingual Meetings

There may be no greater barrier to communication between educators and parents than a language barrier. This problem only increases when several different languages are spoken within one school district, especially when it comes to holding meetings for all parents.

Previously, schools have handled this problem by holding meetings in different languages on different nights or by having interpreters translate after the English-speaking presenter has spoken. These methods, however, can be very time-consuming—especially when several different languages are spoken in a school district.

One school district in central California addressed these problems when it began using a device called a Stenomask. This device, which is typically used by court reporters, allows the user to speak into a microphone that is imbedded into a mask. With minimal training, the speaker's voice can be completely silenced to anyone beyond a foot away. During a school meeting, the translators could talk into the mask, translating what was being said without disrupting other people. Audience members with receivers and earphones could hear the translators' voices without disturbing those around them. This system, also known as the TALK System (TS), accommodates up to 5 different frequencies, thereby allowing translators to talk in 5 different languages.

After nearly 2 years of use in the central California school district, TS improved communication between educators and the multilingual population, increased parent involvement, reduced staff time, and dramatically reduced costs. The system costs approximately $1,000, but funding for it may be available through Title I and Title VII. Approximately 25 states now use TS, mainly in parent-teacher and parent education meetings and with bilingual advisory committees. The system is available through Talk, Inc., in Roswell, Georgia.

Increasing Parent Involvement

School staff at the South Bay Union Elementary School District in Imperial Beach, California, faced the challenge of involving diverse ethnic minorities in the school district. The district serves about 10,000 students in grades K–6. Of these students, 62% are Hispanic, 18% are white, 9% are Filipino, and 11% are African American or belong to other minority groups.

Some of the district's strategies for increasing parent involvement included evaluating the superintendent, principals, and teachers on the extent to which they promote and increase parent participation; training staff members on how to interact with and be responsive to parents; offering year-round parenting classes in multiple languages; and providing a parent volunteer coordinator who makes home visits to parents and refers them to social services agencies as needed.

The district's efforts have been successful. The volunteer program hours in a year increased from 103,423 to 130,301. In addition, more than 400 students and 250 parents attended the district's annual Read to Me Conference.

CHAPTER 3

STANDARD II: PARENTING

Definition: Parenting skills are promoted and supported.

PARENTS ARE THEIR CHILDREN'S FIRST and most influential teachers. During school years, children spend only one eighth of their time in school, and parents and caregivers spend more time with their children than any educator. Therefore, the influence parents have on their children's success in school and beyond is tremendous. Despite this great potential, many parents feel inadequately prepared for or overwhelmed by their crucial role. As a result, they often replace spending time *with* their children with spending money *on* their children, showering them with unnecessary material objects. Although it is natural for parents to want to give their children gifts, it is important to remember what civic and political leader Reverend Jesse Jackson, Sr., has said: "Children need your presence, not your presents." Schools need to reinforce this message.

Virtually every job requires and offers some training, except the most important job of all—parenting. Provided with little or no formal preparation, parents must learn their skills "on the job." Today's parents are often separated from extended family members, who in the past provided support in and relief from the stress of child rearing. In addition, many parents have themselves been raised apart from one or both of their own parents, and too often do not know how to build healthy parent-child relationships. Such healthy relationships are what enable children to become caring and responsible members of society, and they are an essential component of successful parent/family involvement programs.

Today's parents need sources of support to build healthy parent-child relationships. Ideally, they should be able to turn to school personnel, program staff, or both, who can then support positive parenting by respecting and affirming the strengths and skills parents need to effectively fulfill their role. As advocates for children, PTA members work with schools to encourage teachers and principals to

- Examine their own assumptions and beliefs about parents' abilities, interests, and values that are based on parents' behavior, ability to communicate, physical appearance, and cultural or economic background

- Take time to get to know the parents of the children they educate, including their history of interactions with the school; values, customs, interests, and talents; child-rearing practices; and worries and dreams for their children

Perhaps Cindy Christopher, an experienced early childhood and elementary teacher, says it best in her 1996 book, *Building Parent/Teacher Communication: An Educator's Guide* (p. 99): "The most important part to remember here is that the parent knows their child better than you do. A year in your classroom does not guarantee you know what is best for each child. . . . Parents are in most cases the most important force in their child's education and life."

RESEARCH FINDINGS

School administrators and educators need to send parents a clear message that "We value you and need your input." They can do this by recognizing parents' roles and responsibilities, asking parents what assistance they need, and working to find ways to meet those needs.

Research by Epstein et al. (1997) supports the fact that valuing and supporting parents often provides many benefits.

Students

- Are more aware of family supervision and gain more respect for parents

- Attend school regularly

- Gain an awareness of education's importance

Parents

- Gain a greater knowledge of the characteristics of childhood and adolescence and have more self-confidence in their parenting abilities

- Become more aware of their own and others' challenges in parenting

Teachers and Administrators

- Gain a greater respect for families' strengths and efforts

- Better understand student and family diversity

- Better understand families' concerns, goals, and needs

QUALITY TIPS FOR SUCCESSFUL PROGRAMS

Although research confirms the importance of supporting parents and promoting parenting skills, it is not always easy to translate research into practice. The suggestions below can help teachers, administrators, and PTA leaders fulfill their obligation to support families and provide them with the information they need to become effective parents.

- Reach out and provide information to all families—not just those who attend parent meetings or workshops.

- Encourage school administrators and educators to demonstrate respect for families and for families' primary role in rearing children to become responsible adults.

PARENTING

- Communicate the importance of positive relationships between parents and their children.

- Link parents to community programs and resources that provide support services to families.

- Establish policies that support and respect family responsibilities, recognizing the variety of parenting traditions and practices found in the diverse cultures and religions of a community.

- Enable families to share information with educators about their backgrounds, cultures, goals, and needs. Find ways to help parents share and value their unique qualities.

- Learn which ethnic groups are represented in your school or program, and provide translation and other support services when needed. Be sensitive to cultural differences and find appropriate ways to communicate acceptance and respect.

- Provide an accessible parent/family information and resource center to support families with training, resources, and other services.

- Affirm parent responsibilities by meeting with parents before providing special services for children, such as counseling or other social services.

THE ROLES PARENTS PLAY

Parents can play four basic roles in their children's lives and education. The National PTA believes that parents have a right and a responsibility to safeguard and nurture the physical, social, and spiritual education of their children and to lay the foundation for responsible citizenship. To support and encourage all parents to adopt and play every role, school staff, teachers, and administrators must find ways to support and help parents become effective in each of the following four roles (adapted from Henderson & Berla, 1995, and Lueder, 1998).

TEACHERS/NURTURERS—This role focuses on parents' involvement in their children's physical, moral, intellectual, emotional, and social development. Parents can nurture this development by providing an environment for children that promotes learning and develops the skills and values needed to become physically, psychologically, and emotionally healthy adults.

COMMUNICATORS/ADVISORS—Establishing effective two-way communication between the home and the school is the key task of this role. Parents must also maintain open communication with their children in order to counsel them on personal and educational issues, as explored in chapter 2. This chapter focuses on how parents can help school staff, teachers, and administrators understand their families and how parent education programs need to communicate with all types of families.

SUPPORTERS/LEARNERS—This role focuses on parents obtaining skills and knowledge that will assist them with their children's educational and social development. In turn, parents can contribute their knowledge and skills to the school by enriching the curriculum and providing services and support to students and teachers. This role will be explored further in chapters 4 and 5.

COLLABORATORS/DECISION MAKERS—In this role, parents participate with school administrators and educators to help solve problems, make decisions, and develop policies that make the school system more responsive and equitable to all families. This can be accomplished by parents serving on advisory councils, site-based management teams, curriculum committees, and so forth. This role will be discussed in chapter 6.

PTAS, PARENT EDUCATORS, AND SCHOOLS WORKING TOGETHER

Supporting Parents as Teachers/Nurturers

Supporting parents as first educators is not easy. A parent's job is complex, and effective parenting takes time, patience, and love. Bill Wagonseller, a professor at the University of Nevada at Las Vegas and a lecturer on effective parenting, states that the "responsibility of being a successful parent is accepting the role of teaching and guiding children as they reach for adulthood" (National School Public Relations Association, 1991, p. 8).

The role of PTA members, parent educators, teachers, administrators, and school staff is to work together with parents to provide them with the knowledge and skills they need to become effective teachers and nurturers. The PTA, in conjunction with parent educators and educators, should provide parent education programs that teach skills for parenting children of all age levels and provide information on developmental stages and milestones, from infancy through the high school years.

In some school communities, parents may need more basic assistance. In these cases, it may be necessary to

- Develop family support programs or make referrals to existing community agencies to help parents make sure students arrive at school rested, fed, clean, and ready to learn

- Help parents build a file on their children that includes medical records, pictures, fingerprints, report cards, and other important information; schools can sponsor photography and fingerprinting programs for children in the community

- Sponsor clothing swaps, food co-ops, coat and boot drives, and neighborhood watch programs

- Provide information on free clinics, immunizations, and doctors and dentists in the community that accept public assistance

DESIGNING PARENTING PROGRAMS. Effective parent education programs should be designed to help parents

- Develop a trusting relationship with their children based on respect and love

- Develop appropriate expectations of their children based on age, developmental abilities, and temperament

- Set clear, appropriate, and consistently enforced limits to provide structure and predictability to their children's worlds

- Practice alternative methods of behavior management through timeouts, privilege systems, logical consequences, and positive reinforcements

- Teach children effective problem-solving skills for resolving conflict

- Give children choices, responsibilities, and opportunities to make decisions, so that they become problem solvers, learn from their mistakes, and are responsible for the consequences of their actions

All parenting programs should have the objectives listed above, but parenting programs that focus on specific areas of development may be even more helpful to parents. Because children in different stages of development have different needs, parents may need additional skills or information on specific areas of development. Several of the specific needs parents may have during the different stages of childhood development are listed below.

Parents of infants need to

- Learn how to accept and respond to unique character traits in infants, such as temperament, needs, and patterns of behavior

- Recognize developmental milestones in an infant's first year of life

- Take safety precautions to prevent common childhood accidents

- Address important health/immunization issues

- Select appropriate toys and learning materials

Parents of toddlers need to

- Understand the normal process of speech and language development and how to identify indicators of potential problems

- Set guidelines for appropriate behavior and practice appropriate discipline

- Understand when toddlers have temper tantrums

- Understand the importance of using books, employing developmentally appropriate activities, and playing to enhance learning

Parents of preschoolers need to

- Understand the children's need to master themselves and their environment

- Provide interactions, such as daily conversations with children, which are important to developing age-appropriate skills

- Build the children's self-esteem and confidence through experiences that allow for responsibility and success; for example, by designing children's rooms with low shelves, coat hooks, and step stools, parents can allow children independent access to toys and other objects

- Understand the importance of play in learning and development

Parents of elementary school-aged children need to

- Understand the importance of peer acceptance to children

- Facilitate children's need to know how things work in the world

- Develop a home environment that supports learning

- Keep a healthy balance between play and extracurricular activities such as soccer, dance classes, and music lessons

- Provide opportunities for children to practice making choices

Parents of middle school-aged children need to

- Understand and support children's growing need for independence

- Talk to children about sex, and help them develop healthy and safe relationships

- Accept, rather than approve of, children's odd and antagonistic behaviors that may challenge the parents' authority

- Offer love and support as children make choices and mistakes during this experimental stage

- Help children prepare for the transition to high school

Parents of teenagers need to

- Accept and help them establish independence and an identity separate from their family and their peers

- Help them establish their own set of values to guide the many choices and decisions they will face

- Help them prepare for college and a future occupation

When schools provide effective and meaningful parent education classes and programs, parents can consciously assume their responsibility and foster the development of a good value system in their children. This helps children become caring, successful, and responsible adults.

Supporting Parents as Communicators/Advisors

In the communicator/advisor role, parents effectively communicate with their own families and help educators understand the parents' families and children. Effective two-way communication can be greatly enhanced by efforts both from parents and from PTA members, parent educators, and school representatives.

PTA members and parent educators can use the following suggestions to help school administrators and educators help parents improve their communication skills:

- Encourage teachers and principals to break down barriers and develop a common bond with parents by sharing experiences they have had with their own children in similar situations.

- Reach out to parents to gain their perspectives on their role as parents.

- Ensure that parent classes, events, and PTA programs and meetings include and are sensitive to the issues faced by a wide spectrum of families (for example, two-career families, single-parent families, blended families, extended families, and grandparents raising children).

Parents can do the following to help school administrators and educators better understand their families:

- Share information (such as family customs, beliefs, child-rearing practices, and how teachers may influence their children's behavior or personality at school) with teachers at the beginning of the school year, during parent-teacher conferences, through phone calls, through notes, and in informal meetings.

- Share with teachers and principals perceptions of how parents are regarded by the school and how this makes them feel.

- Work together to change the perceptions that make parents feel unwelcome, uncomfortable, or devalued.

Because communication is the key to effective parenting, PTAs need to be sure that they are helping to build skills that will enable all parents to effectively communicate and be involved in their children's lives. Although there are many kinds of families to consider, this section will focus only on single-parent families and blended families.

This limited focus is not intended to diminish the importance of parent involvement by two-parent families. According to 1997 Census Bureau statistics, 25% of all children under 18 live with two biological or adoptive parents (Bryson & Casper, 1998, p. 1). It is, therefore, important that PTAs should recognize and meet the growing needs of two-parent, two-career families. Bureau of Labor Statistics research shows that in 1996, there were nearly 4.5 million homes in which two adults each worked two or more jobs (Stinson, 1997, p. 5). Lack of time is a real issue for such families. Therefore, we need to develop more creative programs in order to reach out to these parents. Also, according to the U.S. Census Bureau, in 1996 there were 4 million children living in households headed by grandparents, and nearly 1.5 million of these children had no parent living in the home (U.S. Census Bureau, 1997, p. 2). Lack of support, money, and health insurance for children are issues to address in programs designed to support grandparent-headed households.

SINGLE PARENTS AND DIVORCED PARENTS. Historically, most PTA or parent meetings and parenting programs have focused on the "traditional family," and more specifically the mother within that family. Today's family, however, has many different faces. As the divorce rate increases, there are both more single-parent families and more children being raised by stepparents. Statistics also indicate that young women who become parents tend not to be married. There are now 12.8 million female-headed households, which is an increase of 133% since 1970 (Bryson & Casper, 1998, p. 5). The number of single-parent households headed by fathers is also growing. Currently, there are 2 million single-parent male-headed households, which represents 17% of all households. This is a 33% increase since 1970 (Bryson & Casper, 1998, p. 5).

When parents are divorced, school staff and educators need to make newsletters, report cards, and other school communications available to both parents. School forms should allow parents to indicate how such information should be shared with the other parent. For example, forms could have a box to check that indicates joint custody, single custody, or if a child lives with both parents. If parents check the single custody box, the schools should ask that the noncustodial parent's visitation schedule be included.

PTA members, in conjunction with local professionals, also need to create relevant parent programs that address basic communication and parenting issues faced by all families, especially those in which the parents have divorced. Classes and programs for divorced parents and single parents, for example, should focus on how to deal with the stress and anger that can be involved in a divorce and the challenges of single parenting. Some parenting skills to focus on in designing programs for divorced and single parents include

- Reassuring a child that he or she is not responsible for the situation

- Explaining to children of different ages what a divorce is or why the other parent is not there, positively affirming the parenting role of the absent parent when appropriate

PARENTING

- Avoiding the tendency to condemn the other parent or to make the child the carrier of negative messages between parents

- Helping children find parent substitutes and role models

- Maintaining stability and consistency in the home to provide a sense of security

- Developing a support network and taking care of oneself

These programs also need to focus on the importance of cooperative communication between divorced parents. Children raised in all kinds of family structures deserve to be healthy and happy. Programs should concentrate on helping divorced parents work together to solve problems in ways that best meet the needs of their children. To work out their problems, divorced parents need to talk to each other in a civil manner. Some tips on effective communication between adults include

- Being clear about expectations and needs

- Ensuring that the other parent understands what is being requested

- Identifying and staying focused on issues that need to be discussed

- Focusing on the problem rather than blaming the other person

- Avoiding making assumptions about what you think the other parent wants or feels

- Keeping conversations focused on the present

STEPPARENTS. The issues stepparents face have long been ignored in traditional parenting programs. Whether children live with stepparents or not, these individuals have the extra challenge of gaining affection and acceptance from children who are often resentful and not interested in a relationship with them. Parenting programs that are meaningful to stepparents need to include information on how to

- Get to know stepchildren

- Avoid coming on too strong

- Create time for stepchildren to spend alone with their parent

- Form bonds with stepchildren by developing common interests

- Create a place for stepchildren so that they feel they fit in

- Avoid favoritism of one's own children over stepchildren

- Keep a sense of humor and take care of oneself when being tested by stepchildren

Stepparents can also benefit from adult communication workshops, because they are often dealing with divorced parent issues as well.

PROJECT IDEAS

Ideas for PTAs and the School Community Working Together

PARENT CENTER. Assemble a family resource center. The center should have cozy places to sit and relax as well as shelves containing books, pamphlets, brochures, audio- and videotapes, games, puzzles, magazines, and tip sheets that provide information on a variety of parenting topics. The area can also feature a computer and software, with Internet access to parenting information. Provide beverages, a play area in the center for small children, a telephone, and if possible, a room with laundry facilities and a kitchen. Approach local businesses for donations of equipment, supplies, and software, and convene a committee to oversee development, operation, and review of the center. Advertise the center in your school newsletter, so parents know it is there and what it offers.

INVOLVEMENT AMBASSADORS. Select a parent involvement chairperson for each local PTA who will reach out to parents and get them involved with the school.

INTERACTIVE ACTIVITIES. Provide a toy-lending library, and offer take-home family kits that contain toys, games, books, and informational pamphlets or videos (for example, how to talk to your kids about drugs, sex, etc.). Create interactive bulletin boards, a community resource directory, or a family access network that has parenting articles and information about upcoming school and community family events and lists community-based resources and services for parents.

THE PARENT INSTITUTE. Hold "parent institute" days or "parent fairs" in partnership with community social workers, psychologists, and other experts. Display parenting books, provide handouts and brochures on parenting topics, and offer seminars and workshops for parents on topics such as stress reduction, parent-child communication, child abuse prevention, and adult education. Conduct a survey to find out what topics parents want to have covered in seminars, and where and when parents would like to have the seminars offered.

PARENT CHAT. Start a parent book club to discuss current publications, or host a "VIP" (Very Important Parent) column in the school's newsletter to highlight parenting tips, give real-life examples of how to handle parenting challenges, and provide general information for parents. The newsletter might also include a tear-off form for submitting questions to be answered by a parenting professional in a "Dear _____" column.

Parenting Support for Working Parents

LATCHKEY PROGRAM. Create an after-school program for latchkey children. Provide time for homework, games, and physical activities. Recruit parents who work at home and senior citizen volunteers to organize and staff the program.

TURN YOUR SCHOOL INTO A COMMUNITY CENTER. Keep school facilities, such as the swimming pool and the gymnasium, open for children and families to use after school and in the evenings. Arrange for parent volunteers, teachers, and school support staff to rotate supervision of these areas.

Ideas for Teachers

CELEBRATING PARENTS AS FIRST TEACHERS. Hold a "parents as first teachers" night in your classroom to talk about how parents can function as children's most important teachers by initiating activities such as reading to their children and teaching them problem-solving skills.

TOGETHERNESS ACTIVITIES. Create several half-sheet fliers, each with an activity parents can do with their children (for example, parents talk to children about when they were the child's age, parents read the newspaper with their children, etc.). On the back of the flier, provide information on why the activity is valuable for children and how it supports positive parenting.

PARENTS' BREAKFAST. Hold a Saturday parents' breakfast where teachers and school administrators prepare the meal and serve parents. After breakfast, initiate round-table discussions on important parenting issues.

FAMILY MUSEUM. Begin a "family museum" in your classroom to highlight a particular student's family each week. Send a letter to parents explaining the project and the importance of working on it together with their child as a way of celebrating their family background. The museum might include family histories that parents create with their child by using photographs, scrapbooks, letters, traditional clothing, recipes, maps that trace the family's origin, and so forth.

Ideas for PTAs Working With Middle and High School Communities

PARENT UNIVERSITY. Develop a workshop series for parents that focuses on key issues in adolescence. Topics might include "Building Successful Teens," "Discipline and Environments," "Teen Suicide," and "Talking to Adolescents About Sex." Offer the series on videotape for parents who cannot attend the sessions, or provide highlights from the series in the school newsletter, on a school hotline, or on the school's web page.

MAKING THE CONNECTION. Link parent educational activities with the students' curriculum. For example, while a school program focuses on drugs, parent workshops can focus on learning how to talk with children about drugs.

WELCOME TO PARENTHOOD. With the help of local professionals, offer parenting classes that address the needs of teen parents. Start a mentoring group that provides information on prenatal and postnatal care and lends age-appropriate books, toys, and games to new parents and soon-to-be parents.

PARENTING

SUPPORT FOR SPECIAL PARENTS. Provide parent support groups that allow divorced parents, single parents, teen parents, stepparents, and grandparents the opportunity to share approaches and perspectives on parenting issues, address the special parenting challenges they face, and receive peer support.

PARENT TO PARENT. Facilitate parent-to-parent contacts so that families can meet and get to know each other, become acquainted with their children's friends, and better monitor their children's after-school and social activities.

BEST PRACTICES

Each community and each set of volunteers are unique. These programs should be considered as guidelines. If you think a program might work for you, adapt it to your situation.

Dad's Club

In 1992, the Dad's Club was started and sponsored by an assistant principal and the Parent/Community Involvement Cadre (team) at the Rancho Milpitas Middle School in Milpitas, California. The program offers a fun way for fathers, stepfathers, grandfathers, single fathers, and any man who cares for children to bond with children and other fathers.

The program fits well with the school's vision statement, which calls on fathers to be an important part of students' success. Dad's Club members meet monthly and discuss topics such as how to help their children in all aspects of their lives, how to communicate at home, and how to make their homes into places that support healthy children. They also volunteer in the school office and as classroom aides, and they are active in such events as the science fair and career night. Through the club, the men are involved in father-child activities such as taking children to sporting events and attending parent-teacher conferences.

Since the club's start, the number of men volunteering and assisting in school activities has increased, and some men stay involved even after their children have moved on to high school.

Parent Institute Days

Most schools have teacher institute days for additional teacher training, but the PTA district of Homewood, Illinois, offers Parent Institute Days to provide additional parent training for community members from dozens of local schools.

Since 1990, PTA District 19 has worked with numerous cooperating agencies and education organizations to present Parent Institute Days. Held from Thursday through Saturday, the event includes speakers, community resource exhibits, networking opportunities, keynote speakers, and more than 80 workshops on topics such as drug awareness, special education needs, homework help, and discipline.

Attendees are charged a nominal fee, which covers the cost of a continental breakfast, lunch, and workshop materials. Fees vary, depending on how many workshops or days parents attend, but typically range from $10 to $15.

Parent Institute Days have been a success from the beginning, and the event has only grown in popularity. The first Parent Institute Days attracted about 400 people. Now, the event is held at a local community college in order to accommodate up to 900 attendees.

PERC-olating Parenthood

Children do not come with operating instructions, and parents may sometimes be unsure about where they should turn for parenting information. Some parents in Utah, however, can turn to the Davis County Parent Education Resource Center (PERC) for a wide variety of programs and educational services designed to help parents, professionals, and community agencies.

PERC was formed in the late 1970s to address child-rearing concerns identified in a parent survey sponsored by the Davis County school district and PTA. Since then, PERC has grown to offer parenting programs that help improve parenting skills, strengthen family relationships, increase self-awareness, and teach about children's social, emotional, and academic development.

PERC, which is located in a public school that serves children with physical disabilities, offers a large library of books, toys, films, pamphlets, and kits on child development and parenting. These materials are free to parents and professionals. PERC also offers classes and discussion groups on parenting, and the PERC staff works with community volunteer organizations such as churches and PTAs.

An evaluation of PERC showed that parents' participation in the center significantly increased their knowledge of child development. This evaluation was crucial in obtaining funding from the school district when state funding ended.

SPAN the Gap

Single-parent families are often overlooked among parent-teacher organizations. However, an organization in Honolulu, Hawaii, made a special effort to reach out to this sometimes-forgotten group. This organization, the Single-Parent Family Advocacy Network (SPAN), is a grassroots project formed by a group of social service providers who were aware of the increasing number of single-parent families in the community. In response, SPAN partnered with the YWCA of Oahu to offer an array of advocacy and direct services to single-parent families. SPAN receives its funding from grants from local private trusts and foundations, as well as a local government contract for job training. It offers its services free to any single-parent family in need.

SPAN advocates on behalf of single-parent families to policymakers at all levels of government and presents training and workshops both for single parents and for other agencies and groups working with families. SPAN also has direct services that include an information and resource bank, a monthly newsletter, support groups, workshops, and a number of services for single parents who need help achieving economic self-sufficiency. These services, collectively called WomanFriend, also include support services and classes in self-esteem, parenting, finances, and personal development. SPAN also links parents to job-training programs that give counseling and support.

Reaching out to the community is a crucial part of SPAN's success. It does this by holding neighborhood meetings and workshops in the community and, when appropriate, working directly with families in their homes.

The Family/Work Juggling Act: Resources for Working Parents

Juggling family responsibilities with work responsibilities is a daunting task for many parents. Acknowledging and addressing that challenge is the goal of the Working Family Resource Center, managed by the public school system in St. Paul, Minnesota. The center is located in the heart of downtown St. Paul and offers noontime seminars on a variety of work and family issues, such as managing family and work stress, balancing work and family responsibilities, and coping with changing family demographics. It also offers either complete training programs or individual modules that can be taught at the parents' places of employment. Another service offered by the resource center is assistance for employers who are planning health and wellness fairs.

Visitors to the resource center have access to a library with more than 600 books, periodicals, and videotapes on childcare, child development, school/home communication, parenting, and other issues. Visitors can also consult with a parent involvement educator on any topic relating to balancing work and family.

The resource center was started with a grant, and its continued funding comes from fees and the St. Paul Public Schools Community Education Department. Local businesses donate furniture, books, and equipment, and the office space is donated by the owner of the resource center's building.

Taking Parent Involvement on the Road

When the San Diego schools implemented a formal parent involvement policy, some school staff found themselves going mobile. The San Diego school district is the eighth largest in the U.S. Sixty languages are spoken in the district, and students come from a range of socioeconomic

PARENTING

levels. The student population is 35% white, 29% Latino, 17% Asian American, 16% African American, and 3% other.

As part of their plan to get parents involved, school staff asked for funding for a parent center. Instead, district officials gave them a bus. Deciding that the bus would have to do as the parent center, the staff sent it to a state prison where it was renovated and redesigned. Then the renovated bus was equipped with tables, chairs, a laminator, a copier, pamphlets, and materials parents could check out for home use, such as parenting books, children's books, and educational games. The Mobile Parent Resource Center travels to three to four schools each week and is available to go to any school or neighborhood to which it is invited.

The mobile center also offers a series of two-hour hands-on workshops for parents. The workshops feature topics such as how to have a successful parent-teacher conference, how to communicate with your child, how to build your child's self-esteem, and how to help your child succeed in school. The school staff wants the mobile center to reach out to as many parents as possible.

CHAPTER 4

STANDARD III: STUDENT LEARNING

Definition: Parents play an integral role in assisting student learning.

IN TODAY'S WORLD, ALL CHILDREN NEED HELP from their parents and other caregivers to succeed in school and in life. The hours children spend learning in school, while important, are fewer than the hours they spend at home. The average school year is only 180 days, and the average school day is 6 hours, including lunch and recess. The many hours and days children spend away from school are very important times for learning. In today's competitive society, educators need to support parents in communicating to their children the following positive attitudes about education:

- Learning can be fun and interactive.

- Education is valuable and important.

- Setting high expectations for oneself can help shape one's future.

As Franklin D. Roosevelt once said, "We cannot always build the future for our youth, but we can build our youth for the future."

BARRIERS TO INVOLVING PARENTS IN STUDENT LEARNING AT HOME

It is not always easy for parents to assume the role of helping their children learn. PTA members and school staff, teachers, and administrators need to work together to recognize and overcome some of the obstacles that can prevent this from occurring.

When Teachers and Administrators Misunderstand the Roles Parents Play

PTA members, teachers, and administrators must first understand the roles parents see themselves as occupying in their children's life and education, and how these perceived roles can influence their beliefs and actions. Chapters 2 and 3 discussed two of the four parent roles (teachers/nurturers and communicators/advisors).

The third role, that of supporter/learner, has two parts. The first part of this role is for parents to acquire the skills and knowledge they need so they can assist with their children's educational development. The second part of the role, which will be discussed in the next chapter, focuses on how parents can contribute their knowledge and skills to the school, thereby enriching the curriculum and providing services and support to students and teachers.

Often, parents seem uninterested in or unwilling to assume the role of supporter/learner. When parents do not attend parent-teacher conferences, participate in school events, or help their children with homework, educators may come to believe that these parents are not interested in their children's learning. There are often specific reasons for these absences, however, which educators and PTA members may fail to realize.

The reasons are as varied as the different types of families. For working parents, participating in daytime activities is nearly impossible, and evenings may be the only time they have to spend with their children. Instead of attending school functions, parents may choose to spend this time at home with their family. Other seemingly uninvolved parents may have had a negative school experience of their own, and therefore feel uncomfortable in a school setting. Whatever the reason, it is important that educators and PTA members not make hasty assumptions about the underlying causes of parents' actions or inaction. More can be accomplished by working with parents to increase their participation.

When Parents Misunderstand Their Own Roles

Some parents may feel that their involvement in their children's education should be limited to sending the children to school clean, fed, and with good manners (fulfilling the teacher/nurturer role). Even parents who are confident that they should be actively involved in their children's learning may hesitate to do so for fear of overstepping their bounds. Because promoting learning in the home and expecting parents to "teach" their children at home may appear to blur the lines between the roles of teachers and parents, educators and PTA members must emphasize, in a nonthreatening way, the value of the contributions parents can make with home learning. PTA members and educators must provide the information and tools parents need to help them feel confident about becoming involved in their children's education.

When Educators and Parents Make the Wrong Assumptions

Another barrier to parents adopting the third role of supporter/learner is an erroneous assumption on the part of both parents and educators that parents are not *able* to help their children succeed in school. Educators may assume that some parents cannot help their children with homework because of the parents' own inadequate education background. This assumption does a great disservice to both parents and students.

Many parents believe they cannot be of much assistance in their children's learning. While the vast majority of them are willing to assist their children, they often are unsure what assistance would be most helpful and appropriate. Parents may also not know much about the curriculum, education jargon, technology, expectations, or grading systems of their children's school. This results in their feeling unable to effectively support their children's learning.

Another incorrect assumption many parents make is that their children's school and learning experiences are similar to what they experienced when they were children. For example, without having visited a classroom since their own school days, parents may remember it as a place of rigid rules and high expectations, with little tolerance for failure. School may not be viewed as an enjoyable experience but rather as a requirement. In these parents' perception, contact with the school can only mean there are problems concerning their children, and therefore it is not something they want to be involved in.

Research has proven that if parents are valued and perceived as able to help their children academically, they are much more likely to be actively involved, regardless of their socioeconomic status or level of education (Lewis & Henderson, 1997; U.S. Department of Education, 1997). Because this active involvement leads to an increase in student learning, it is of paramount importance to explain the value of this role to parents.

Cultural Differences

Misperceptions about schools and parents' roles in education can become an ever-greater barrier for families of different ethnic backgrounds. Families who do not speak fluent English or who have been raised and educated in another country may have an even more difficult time understanding the curriculum and expectations of their children's school. These families may have an especially hard time understanding how they can facilitate their children's learning at home. To help parents overcome these barriers and become active participants in their children's learning, school staff and teachers must make sincere efforts to translate materials, provide workshops in other languages, and pair parents who do not speak fluent English with bilingual parents.

To remove old perceptions and break persistent cycles of relationships between home and school, there needs to be an active shift in thinking and attitudes among educators. By enlisting parents' assistance, PTAs can be influential in providing teachers and administrators with a valuable support system for creating a team that works together for each child's success.

To connect the school to the home, PTA members must work with educators to develop programs that focus on the success of all students, that serve the whole child, and that share the responsibility with parents for student success.

RESEARCH FINDINGS

Research reinforces the idea that valuing and supporting parents as key figures in their children's learning often provides the following benefits (Epstein et al., 1997):

Students

- Develop self-confidence in their ability as learners

- Develop a positive attitude toward homework and school

- Get higher grades and test scores, have better attendance, and complete homework more consistently

Parents

- Are more knowledgeable of how to support and encourage their children at home

- Understand the curriculum and what their children are learning in school

- Discuss children's school day, homework, and class work more regularly

Teachers and Administrators

- Recognize the importance of families in motivating and reinforcing student learning

- Create more interactive homework assignments for parents and children to do together

- Respect families' time more

STUDENT LEARNING

Conditions in the Home Associated With School Success

Research also confirms the following five positive conditions that can be created at home to influence children's learning (Kellaghan, Sloane, Alvarez, & Bloom, 1993; National PTA, National Association of Elementary School Principals, & World Book, 1991; National PTA & World Book, 1993):

1. Family work habits

2. Academic guidance and support

3. Participation in activities to stimulate exploration and discussion

4. Language development and environment

5. Academic ambitions and expectations

FAMILY WORK HABITS. Good family work habits can influence school performance. Children can do better in school when parents provide a time for work and play at home, give priority to schoolwork and reading before recreation, and adhere to a structure of sharing and punctuality in home activities. By teaching time management and organization skills, school administrators and educators can help parents understand the importance of establishing structure and planning routines. School administrators and educators can also help parents understand the importance of allowing children to share responsibilities at home. Planning and completing routines for studying, chores, and play can help children set goals, follow through on plans, and accomplish projects or tasks.

ACADEMIC GUIDANCE AND SUPPORT. Learning is a lifelong process. Along the way, every child encounters some difficulties in particular areas. The home needs to be a place of encouragement and support to help children to overcome these difficulties and maintain a commitment to learning (Office of Educational Research and Improvement, 1998). Parents need to show an interest in and support for their children's learning to demonstrate that they believe education is important. PTA members and educators can help parents learn how to do this by providing information and support from teachers and by conducting workshops and PTA meetings that focus on the following topics and strategies:

Providing Encouragement

- Give frequent encouragement and approval for good school-work.

- Tell others about your children's accomplishments, and display their work at home.

- Be there for children, even if it is through phone calls.

Knowing Children's Strengths and Weaknesses in Learning

- Find out what children are learning in school and what the expectations of teachers are each year.

- Know children's strengths and weaknesses in each area of the school's curriculum.

- Become acquainted with children's learning styles and with how they best receive and process information.

- Encourage children to explain their assignments and share what they are learning in school.

- Develop a method for exchanging information between teachers and parents on a regular basis.

Creating an Appropriate Environment for Learning

- Provide a quiet place to work at home (such as a desk or table) away from the television.

- Minimize noise and provide adequate lighting for studying.

- Supply materials (such as paper, pencils, pens, erasers, a dictionary, and a thesaurus) to help with homework and studying.

Developing Good Study Skills

- Help children set a consistent time each day to study.

STUDENT LEARNING

- Talk with children about their assignments, and work through problems together to make sure they understand what they need to do.

- Develop a system of recording when assignments are due and organizing a timeline for completing tasks.

- Break down large or long-term projects into manageable steps.

- Help children see how much time is needed to complete each step and what the logical sequence of steps should be. (For example, the steps for a written report might include going to the library to do research, taking notes, developing an outline, writing each section of the report, and so forth.)

- Develop creative ways to help children review important material and take effective notes in class.

PARTICIPATION IN ACTIVITIES TO STIMULATE EXPLORATION AND DISCUSSION. Family activities, hobbies, games, and visits to places in the community can be opportunities to help children grow and to reinforce the concepts that are being taught in school. PTA members and teachers can work together to provide information to families in the following areas:

Pursuing Family Interests and Activities

- Learn how to share interests in hobbies (i.e., gardening, fixing cars) with children, and turn these interactions into learning experiences.

- Learn how to turn daily routine activities such as setting the table, taking a bath, cooking, and putting away groceries into fun and interactive learning experiences for young children. (These types of activities can be used to teach about the colors, shapes, and sizes of objects, as well as to teach beginning math skills such as counting, sorting, and measurement.)

Using Reading Materials and the TV

- Provide children with access to printed materials, such as newspapers, magazines, and books.

- Develop nighttime reading routines with children that include reading out loud, asking questions, and discussing books.

- Establish strategies for viewing daily events, news, and selected programs together, and discuss them at home and in class.

Engaging in Cultural Activities

- Work with the public library to provide workshops for families on the programs and services the library provides (for example, how to get a library card, how to use the facility, how to participate in special programs).

- Make visits to museums, zoos, historical sites, parks, the backyard, and walks through the neighborhood into fun learning experiences for children.

- Sponsor interactive family learning nights at school that focus on a specific area of the arts such as music or painting.

- Encourage listening and playing different styles of music, and help children learn creatively by producing or going to see art, plays, films, and dance performances.

LANGUAGE DEVELOPMENT AND ENVIRONMENT. So much of education depends on the ability to listen, read, and express ideas clearly—both verbally and in writing. Therefore, parents' emphasis on enriching language, developing vocabulary, and improving reading is vital. PTA leaders or other parent leaders can help educators encourage parents to do this at home by providing information and strategies for parents to do the following:

- Help children use the correct words and phrases needed to communicate with others.

- Talk to children during daily routines.

- Promote conversation at the dinner table, giving everyone a chance to talk and be heard.

- Encourage children to read to family members, tell them stories, and make up songs.

- Encourage children to write letters, words, and stories. Younger children can dictate stories or write their marks on paper for parents to read.

ACADEMIC AMBITIONS AND EXPECTATIONS. Home is where children learn to reach higher goals and aspire to do their best in school and in the future. Children cannot do this without their parents' or other family members' support and encouragement. PTA members can work together with schools to help parents do the following:

- Set high, but realistic, standards and expectations for learning and performance, and help children meet them.

- Help children aim high, set goals, and have confidence in themselves.

- Help children make plans for the future by doing the following:

  1. Talk with children about what they want to do when they grow up and what skills they need to achieve their goals.

  2. Help children see how their current learning is related to their future ambitions.

  3. Help children make plans to attend high school, college, or vocational or trade school.

  4. Attend college and career expositions with children.

Practicing What We Preach

As important as it is to create home conditions that promote learning, it is equally important to create such conditions at school. Educators must ensure that their classrooms reflect the kind of environment that promotes the type of learning they expect. Classrooms that enable students to be independent thinkers and active learners include

- Frequent teacher/student and student/student interaction

- Students asking questions and making choices

- Students doing projects, finding information, working together in small groups, and experimenting with a variety of materials

- Problem solving and critical thinking, rather than just memorizing information and facts

- Extra help from other students, tutors, and teachers in needed areas

QUALITY TIPS FOR SUCCESSFUL PROGRAMS

Whether they are displaying student work at home or responding to a particular class assignment, parents' actions can show their children that education is important. Schools need to teach parents effective strategies for helping their children learn. The following list offers teachers, administrators, and PTA members some suggestions to help strengthen the connection among parents, school staff, and children:

- Seek and encourage parent participation in decision making that affects students.

- Inform parents of expectations for students in each subject at each grade level.

- Provide information on how parents can foster learning at home, give appropriate assistance, monitor homework, and give feedback to teachers.

- Assign interactive homework on a regular basis that requires students to discuss and interact with their parents about what they are learning in class.

- Sponsor workshops or distribute information that helps parents understand how students can improve skills, get help when needed, meet class expectations, and perform well on assessments.

- Provide information to help parents understand assessment and grading procedures.

- Involve parents in setting student goals each year and in planning for postsecondary education and careers. Encourage the development of a personalized education plan for each student, including the parents as full partners in the effort.

- Provide opportunities for educators to learn and share successful strategies for engaging parents in their children's education.

PROJECT IDEAS

Ideas for PTAs and the School Community Working Together

MEDIA BLITZ. Publicize ways for parents to support student learning by creating posters that display tips. Include in each school newsletter a "Did You Know?" column that highlights research on how parent involvement affects student achievement. You might also encourage the local newspaper to run articles on parent involvement in student learning.

GETTING THE RIGHT TOOLS FOR THE JOB. Hold a community drive or seek donations from businesses to supply materials such as folders, pens, pencils, erasers, paper, and dictionaries for children whose parents cannot provide necessary school supplies.

FAMILY LEARNING NIGHTS. Sponsor a series of learning sessions, such as family math, science, or reading nights, for both parents and children. During these sessions, provide parents with an overview of what students will be learning in different curriculum areas, how they will be assessed, the grade-level expectations, and how they can learn to improve grades and study habits. Include hands-on learning activities, suggestions for parents on questions to ask, and beneficial ways to practice counting, spelling, and so forth. Recommending that a parent should attend with the student can increase the influence of these sessions.

DIGITAL-AGE PARENTS. Contact local businesses for sponsorship and funding to create a computer-lending library. Sponsor family technology nights where parents learn how to use the school's computers, software, and the Internet to assist children's learning. Allow parents to take home personal computers and software. Establish acceptable use policies for Internet and e-mail use by students. Explain these policies to parents and children, and have both sign the policies sheet.

PORTFOLIO REVIEWS. Invite parents to help teachers organize portfolio reviews as part of parent-teacher conference night. This gives parents the chance to review project expectations, discover their children's areas of strength, and gain insights into how to help their children improve. PTA members or parent leaders could promote the event, contact other parents, and coordinate these sessions. Teachers would conduct the review sessions.

Ideas for Teachers

PLANNING FOR SUCCESS. Meet with parents at the beginning of the school year (the first parent-teacher conference) to discuss and agree on an individual learning plan for each student. The plan should meet the student's needs and sets goals for his or her progress to be evaluated throughout the year at subsequent parent-teacher conferences.

BINGO! Distribute a bingo-like card, with each box containing a parent activity that supports student learning. Have families initial each activity as they do it. Families that have initialed all the activities on the card by the end of the term receive a certificate and some kind of recognition, such as coupons or certificates for local stores or restaurants.

TAKE-HOME LEARNING. Seek donations to create exploration kits for families and students. The kits should support learning activities and offer a way for parents and children to explore an academic subject together. They might contain videos, books, writing supplies, learning toys, or games on a particular subject area, as well as activities, pertinent questions to ask, and a communication log for parents to comment on the benefits of using the kit. Teachers could circulate the kits among the students, make them available at parent-teacher conferences, or make them a part of the family resource center for parents to check out.

FAMILY PROJECTS. Assign projects that readily lend themselves to involving parents or other family members. These might include personal interviews on specific topics, reports based on family activities, or visits to community museums or points of interest. Provide advance instructions and specific guidelines for each project, and offer a short list of checkpoints for parents to respond to after the assignment. For example:

❑ My child understands and correctly applies this skill.

❑ My child needed help on this, but overall seems to understand this lesson.

❑ My child needs further instruction on this skill/lesson.

TEACHING PARENTS TO TEACH. Invite parents to in-service programs to learn new curriculum and teaching methods along with the teachers. Hold workshops on creating home-learning materials by using everyday items and routines to create educational games and learning opportunities.

Ideas for PTAs Working With Middle and High School Communities

The shift to middle or high school is difficult for most students and families. When parents remain involved in daily activities and schoolwork, however, children make a better adjustment and are much more likely to graduate and go on to postsecondary education (Henderson & Berla, 1995). Educators, administrators, and school staff can assist families through these transitions, and help them stay involved, with the following strategies.

LUNCH JAMS. Encourage principals to schedule brown-bag lunch sessions for parents at a major community employer. Have principals show slides of the school, talk about its mission, and discuss goals and concerns for children.

ACADEMIC FOCUS NIGHTS. Focus high school family learning nights around a particular academic discipline, such as math or science. Teachers from various courses could conduct sessions, giving tips on how to achieve in their particular classes. In addition, students could teach their parents about learning strategies through stories, games, graphing, and patterns. These nights could be geared toward an individual class or grade level.

KEEPING PARENTS IN THE LOOP. Keep parents informed by giving them a syllabus and a written copy of class expectations for each of their children's classes. Also, give parents monthly planners to help students organize their assignments and activities, and designate a teacher-advisor for a group of students who can keep parents informed of placement decisions, course choices, and their effect on students' future options.

STUDENT MENTORS. Start a community mentoring program that pairs young children with high school or college students who can assist them with special needs or provide enrichment and special resources to nurture their talents. Check with local community organizations, churches, and universities or colleges for similar programs that are already available.

LEARNING CELEBRATIONS. With careful adult supervision, hold history and literary fairs and student film festivals. At a history fair, students and parents can select a country and work together to design a booth or display, make presentations, and hold discussions on the country. For a literary fair, host a literary costume contest, perform student written plays and stories, give puppet shows, participate in carnival games to promote reading skills, or hold a library card sign-up drive. Host a student film festival that shows student made films and includes discussion of the social values and issues that are dealt with in the films.

"WHERE DO I GO FROM HERE?" NIGHT. Host a college and vocational fair for parents and students. Invite local businesses to attend and provide information to students and parents about available opportunities. Invite postsecondary guidance and financial aid counselors, as well as presidents of student organizations, to talk to students about what to expect and about how to make course choices, apply for financial aid, join social or academic clubs, seek employment, and look for housing. Provide parents and students with access to the career center.

BEST PRACTICES

Each community and each set of volunteers are unique. These programs should be considered as guidelines. If you think a program might work for you, adapt it to your situation.

STUDENT LEARNING

TIPS for Student Learning

It can be hard for parents to feel involved in their children's learning when they don't know what students are doing in class. A program called Teachers Involve Parents in Schoolwork (TIPS) can help to get parents, students, and teachers talking to each other. TIPS is based on the *Manual for Teachers and Prototype Activities: Teachers Involve Parents in Schoolwork (TIPS) Language Arts, Science/Health, and Math Interactive Homework in the Elementary Grades/Middle Grades, and Prototype Activities* (Epstein & Clark-Salinas, 1997).

The program's focus is on assigning homework that requires students to talk to someone at home about what they are learning in class. Students must do their own homework, but parents can help by checking students' work and learning along with them. When homework becomes a three-way partnership among the student, teacher, and parent, lines of communication are opened and parents become more involved in their children's progress in school. Furthermore, TIPS requires no extra staffing, and the main cost of the program is in copying homework assignments for students.

Researchers for the Center on School, Family, and Community Partnerships (www.csos.jhu.edu/p2000) at Johns Hopkins University worked with teachers to develop homework that helps students practice, create, discover, and communicate skills and ideas. They have developed homework in language arts, science, and health for students in grades 6–8. Science and health homework includes topics such as physical and emotional changes in children ages 10–14, drugs, HIV/AIDS, human reproduction, and good eating habits. The center also tells teachers and principals how to develop, use, and evaluate TIPS homework.

A Skills Center That Works

Sometimes getting students ready for the work world takes more resources than one school can offer. In 1983 eight school districts serving 17 high schools in Clark County, Washington, came together, along with many Clark County businesses, to form a cooperative center called the Clark County Skills Center. The center has 13 different programs for high school students. The programs teach a diverse array of skills, from diesel technology to dental assistant training.

A 10-year follow-up study of the center showed that 94% of its graduates either went on to higher education or successful entry-level employment. The students' success is due to many factors, including the instructors' expertise. The center's 13 full-time instructors all have a minimum of 5 years' experience in their instruction areas.

Another factor is the support of county businesses. More than 200 businesses and employers work with the center, giving it time, money, and materials, and offering jobs to its graduates. The center's staff also makes a strong effort to reach out to parents and other community members. Before the school year starts, parents are invited into the center to see how it works, and the staff keeps parents informed through progress reports and a quarterly newsletter. The staff also meets with counselors and administrators from all the participating schools, as well as with state legislators and community organization members.

In 11 years, the center has trained approximately 7,000 students. Its funding has come from businesses and the state government.

FOCUSing on Students

Since 1994, community and PTA members have been helping struggling students succeed at William McKinley Middle School in Cedar Rapids, Iowa, through a parent volunteer program called FOCUS. A parent volunteer started the program, with the help of school administrators, to assist students who did not qualify for special services but were having difficulty with the elementary-to-middle school transition and were not doing well in school.

A tutoring program staffed by parent volunteers, FOCUS meets during a regular class period each school day. While in the program, students receive one-on-one help from tutors on organizational skills, homework, and classroom lessons.

A point system is used to track students' progress and determine their FOCUS grade. Students earn one point for completing a planner of their daily schedules and homework assignments; one point for each regular class assignment completed during the FOCUS program; one point for completing each FOCUS assignment, which can be done only after they have finished their regular class assignments; and one point for social skills, which include positive interaction between tutors and students. A student must receive a minimum of three points per day and 15 points per week to be eligible to participate in special class activities, such as field trips.

The FOCUS coordinator meets weekly, and sometimes daily, with teachers to discuss students' progress and what the teachers are doing in their regular classrooms. Twice each quarter, the coordinator and staff conduct a formal review of student progress.

Learning in a FLASH

Many parents at Crestwood Elementary School in Chesterfield County, Virginia, have new teaching skills, thanks to a series of one-hour workshops, called Project FLASH (Families Learning at School and Home), held in the evenings at the school. Crestwood serves a culturally diverse population and houses county special education programs for students with mental and/or emotional disabilities.

The FLASH program is a joint effort of the school's principal, reading specialist, and PTA, and is free to all Crestwood students and their families. PTA members publicize the program by producing brochures and reminder fliers for families; providing press releases, photographs, and videotapes for the PTA newsletter and local media; and using a telephone tree to remind parents about upcoming workshops.

The program has expanded from 7 workshops to 17, with each workshop serving approximately 100 participants. Workshop topics are drawn from the disciplines of reading, writing, math, science, and nature, and the materials and methods used in the workshops are the same methods used by Crestwood teachers in their classrooms. In a workshop evaluation form, parents said that they felt better equipped to help their children with the subject matter covered in the workshops, and that they would recommend the workshops to other parents.

Another advantage of the program is that it often attracts parents and volunteers who do not typically participate in other PTA-sponsored activities.

A second element of the FLASH program is a before-school tutoring program for at-risk students. Parents meet before school with the tutor and their child for social and academic experiences. This provides these students with one half day of additional schooling per week. Quarterly evaluations of the program show significant student gains.

Local businesses and organizations contribute to Project FLASH's success. Volunteers from the school district, the county, other local education organizations, and the state have assisted with FLASH workshops, and local businesses have donated printing services and refreshments.

Dropping in on Success

Students at Mt. Lebanon Senior High School in Pittsburgh, Pennsylvania, know they always have a place to go when they need some academic help. Hundreds of students find help at the parent-run Study Center, which is open 5 days a week throughout the day until 4:30 p.m.

Located in the school, the Study Center is run by approximately 16 Parent-Teacher-Student Association (PTSA) parent and community volunteers, along with an average of 65 National Honor Society student volunteers. With only a $500 annual budget, the center is made possible by these volunteers. The center offers tutoring, organization and study skills, study tools such as test study planners and verb conjugation practice sheets for foreign languages, proctoring for students who need to take makeup tests, and tutoring in English as a second language. In addition, any study center student who has increased any class grade, except gym, during the quarter receives a free breakfast at the PTSA waffle breakfast.

STUDENT LEARNING

CHAPTER 5

STANDARD IV: VOLUNTEERING

*Definition: Parents are welcome in the school,
and their support and assistance are sought.*

PARENT INVOLVEMENT IN EDUCATION has recently received much attention. Department of Education Secretary Richard W. Riley has identified it as one of the top 10 critical education initiatives, and the Goals 2000: Educate America Act includes it as one of its eight national education goals.

Marian Wright Edelman, founder and director of the Children's Defense Fund, describes parent involvement and volunteer service as "the rent we pay for living. It is the very purpose of life and not something you do in your spare time."

This chapter returns to the role of supporter/learner that parents play in children's lives. The last chapter's discussion of this role focused on how parents could obtain skills and knowledge from the school to help children learn at home. This chapter will examine the second half of the role, which is how parents can enrich the learning environment at school by contributing their knowledge and skills and providing services and support to students and teachers.

RESEARCH FINDINGS

Parents and other adults perform literally millions of dollars worth of volunteer services each year in the public schools. When parents volunteer, families and schools often reap benefits that can be obtained in few other ways. Research reinforces the fact that welcoming parents into the school and seeking their support and assistance can benefit everyone (Epstein et al., 1997).

Students

- Gain a variety of skills and knowledge taught by volunteers

- Learn skills that help them communicate with adults

- Appreciate the talents and contributions of parents and community volunteers

Parents

- Feel welcomed and valued at school

- Gain self-confidence in their ability to be role models for children

- Better understand the teacher's role and responsibilities

Teachers and Administrators

- Gain an awareness of and appreciation for parents' talents and interests

- Learn how to organize, train, and effectively use volunteers

- Have more time to devote individual attention to students

BARRIERS TO SUCCESSFUL SCHOOL VOLUNTEERING

If all the major players agree that volunteers are effective, beneficial, and bring increased resources to the school, why aren't there more successful volunteer programs at schools? Studies have shown that many barriers interfere with providing more successful volunteer opportunities (Baker, 1996; Campbell-Lehn, 1997). Although the study results described below focus on parents, teachers, and principals, most of them can also be applied to PTAs.

Confidentiality

Principals and teachers were consistently concerned with their volunteers' ability to maintain confidentiality. Volunteers, on the other hand, repeatedly expressed the need to be better informed and trained on school policies in order to feel more confident in their roles. Teachers and administrators need to work with parents to find a balance that allows everyone to feel comfortable. Furthermore, educators need to provide an example in this area by not discussing confidential information about students in places such as the staff lounge.

Discipline

In schools that believe in sharing student discipline responsibilities with volunteers, principals and teachers repeatedly expressed disappointment in volunteers' unwillingness to discipline children appropriately. Volunteers, however, consistently felt that little to no direction had been provided on their authority in this area or the type of discipline that they were expected to use in different situations.

Volunteer Assignments

Teachers and principals often felt that parents wanted to volunteer only in their own children's classrooms and, as a result, often limited volunteer assignments to weekly classroom duties during daytime hours. Parents, however, reported feeling limited in their assignments and not valued or needed in other areas of the school. Working parents often felt particularly limited, because school educators did not make scheduling accommodations that allowed these parents to participate in volunteer activities outside of their work hours.

Recruitment

Many teachers and principals believed that if parents were interested in volunteering, they would come forward on their own. Many parents, on the other hand, felt that more efforts should be made to recruit them for assignments that matched their skills and interests.

VOLUNTEERING

QUALITY TIPS FOR SUCCESSFUL PROGRAMS

The following suggestions can help overcome these barriers to creating meaningful and valuable volunteer programs:

- Survey parents about their interests, talents, and availability. Include options for volunteering on the survey; then coordinate the parent resources with those that exist within the school and among the faculty.

- Survey teachers to find out how they would like to employ parents' talents.

- Ensure that volunteer activities are meaningful and built on volunteer interests and abilities.

- Ensure that office staff greetings, signs near the entrances, and other interactions with parents create a climate in which volunteers feel valued and welcomed.

- Educate and assist staff members in creating an inviting climate and effectively using volunteer resources.

- Ensure that parents who are unable to volunteer in the school building are given options for helping in other ways, such as from home or at work.

- Develop a system for staying in touch with all parent volunteers as the year progresses.

- Organize an easy, accessible system for coordinating the efforts of parent volunteers, a system that also provides ample training on volunteer procedures and school protocol.

- Design opportunities for those with limited time and resources to participate by addressing child-care, transportation, and work schedule needs.

- Show appreciation for parents' participation, and value their diverse contributions.

- Develop a system for continually evaluating the parent-volunteer program.

Parents, principals, and teachers all agree that just as communication barriers stand in the way of successful programs, so does the lack of volunteer coordination and administration of such programs by schools. This is an excellent opportunity for an organization based on volunteer participation—such as a PTA—to step up and take the lead. In the ideal situation, PTAs would work with the superintendent and school board and encourage them to formally endorse a school volunteer program. This type of support can give the program additional prestige in the community.

Support can come in the form of developing a written policy on parent/volunteer involvement (this is examined further in chapter 9). PTA members might also ask the school board to hire an outside professional to be a district administrator of all school volunteer programs within a district. Because such an administrator's position requires a great deal of work, it should be a paid position, not one that is filled on a volunteer basis by a PTA member. However, PTA members may need to work with school administrators to find money in the school district's budget to allocate for this position.

SEVEN STEPS TO A SUCCESSFUL VOLUNTEER PROGRAM

The program administrator should work with and train either PTA volunteer coordinators or paid coordinators at local schools. These local school coordinators could then train and lead individual school teams. An individual school team could be composed of several PTA members and school staff, and the team should work with the principal to implement the following seven steps for creating a successful program:

1. Assess volunteer needs at school.

2. Work with and train principals, teachers, and school staff on effectively using and supervising volunteers.

3. Set goals and objectives for volunteer assignments.

4. Recruit volunteers.

5. Train and orient volunteers.

6. Retain and recognize volunteers.

7. Evaluate volunteer performance and program success.

(Steps adapted from *Successful Volunteer Systems,* Great Lakes Resource Access Project, 1991, and *Volunteer-a-Thon,* Wisconsin Department of Public Instruction, 1993.)

Assess Volunteer Needs at School

Volunteer coordinators or teams need to meet regularly with the teachers and staff members who will work most closely with the volunteers. Teacher and staff involvement and commitment are crucial to the inception and long-term success of any volunteer program. Volunteer coordinators or teams need to

- Discuss with educators the merits of volunteers and address concerns and potential problems that may develop among school staff, teachers, and volunteers

- Survey teachers, principals, and other school staff to determine where, besides classrooms, volunteers could work (see Appendix B for examples of surveys)

Volunteers can help in a variety of places, including the following:

- **IN THE OFFICE.** Volunteers can answer phones, assist parents, write grants, order supplies, file papers, create databases and spreadsheets, or design pages on the school's website.

- **ON THE BUS.** Volunteers can serve as bus monitors or aides and/or walk children to and from the bus.

- **IN AND AROUND SCHOOL BUILDINGS.** Volunteers can repair furniture and playground equipment, fix plumbing or electrical problems, or landscape the grounds.

- **ON THE PLAYGROUND.** Volunteers can teach sports and games, or help build a fence or playground equipment, such as a sandbox.

- **AT SPECIAL EVENTS OR PROGRAMS.** Volunteers can plan parties, provide child care, conduct arts and crafts activities, direct school plays, tutor students, help with science projects in after-school programs, or organize toy libraries, parent resource centers, and clothing and food drives.

- **IN WORKSHOPS.** Volunteers can speak on a variety of topics to other parents at community groups, service clubs, Girl Scout or Boy Scout troops, and so forth.

- **IN THE KITCHEN.** Volunteers can plan menus, make snacks, serve meals, and conduct special cooking projects with classrooms.

- **AT HOME.** Volunteers can prepare mailings, sew costumes or draperies for plays, create learning materials for the classroom, tape-record stories or music, or design forms, newsletters, and fliers on a home computer.

Once you have surveyed school staff and teachers to identify their needs, survey parents to identify their talents, interests, and skills. This dual survey method provides the most accurate way to develop relevant and meaningful opportunities for parents to volunteer.

Work With and Train Principals, Teachers, and School Staff on Effectively Using and Supervising Volunteers

A principal can serve as the overall supervisor of a school's volunteer program. PTAs then can work with the principal, encouraging him or her to

- Inform staff and teachers about the mission of the volunteer program and enlist their support

- Make space, such as a restroom or lounge, available to volunteers, and foster a receptive and warm climate for them

- Hold meetings with volunteers and staff to create team spirit

- Help provide training to teachers and staff on using and supervising volunteers

VOLUNTEERING

Few teacher preparation programs in colleges include training on involving parents. Only 14 states require some training in this area for elementary certification, and only 6 states require these kinds of courses for secondary certification (Lewis & Henderson, 1997, p. 16). Therefore, providing adequate training to principals and working with teachers to teach them the appropriate roles, uses, and supervision of volunteers is essential for a successful volunteer program.

Although many teachers feel that they are overworked, they may still be reluctant to accept volunteer help if they think of volunteers as an extra burden. Teachers may also feel that their competency or ability to maintain control of their classrooms will be challenged by a volunteer's presence. To counteract these fears, principals need to work with PTA volunteer coordinators or teams to familiarize teachers with the following guidelines for working with volunteers:

Effectively Using Volunteers

- Anticipate the information volunteers will need to complete their assigned duties, such as signing in, finding materials, setting up an activity, and following basic rules and management procedures.

- Prepare specific and clearly defined tasks for volunteers, and assign them to a designated place in the classroom or office.

- Make sure volunteers understand the importance of the tasks you assign in terms of the school's goals and objectives.

- Get to know volunteers. Encourage them to help plan activities or make suggestions based on their talents and interests.

- Let volunteers observe your techniques and assist you when you demonstrate an activity or complete a task that they will be responsible for doing later on.

Supervising Volunteers

- Set aside a regular time each week to plan with each volunteer.

- Give directions and explanations in nontechnical terms, and always speak with respect to volunteers.

- Avoid assigning responsibilities to volunteers that they are not trained or prepared to do.

- Give credit when it is due, and provide positive feedback and encouragement to volunteers for their contributions and progress.

- Prepare and inform others in the school on what volunteers will be doing. Reinforce their importance, and accept them as legitimate co-workers.

- Introduce volunteers to the school staff or students with whom they will be working.

- Discuss any concerns regarding a volunteer's punctuality or performance as they occur. Request the principal or volunteer coordinator's help in resolving concerns only after a teacher or a school staff member has attempted to resolve the problem with the volunteer.

Set Goals and Objectives for Volunteer Assignments

To ensure a successful volunteer program and long-term involvement by the volunteers, it is important that assignments are carefully selected and are productive, meaningful, and closely matched to volunteers' interests, skills, and motivation for volunteering. Because volunteers want to feel that their jobs are valued and important, PTA volunteer coordinators, teachers, and school staff need to work together to develop creative and specific job descriptions for volunteers.

A job description not only gives a volunteer a clear idea of what is expected, but it also clearly defines and clarifies the job for the staff who will train, work with, and supervise the volunteer (Campbell-Lehn, 1998). When staff members, teachers, and volunteers understand what each of the others do, they are more likely to see how their work benefits the school and its students and how to work together to achieve mutual goals.

VOLUNTEERING

A clear and meaningful job description should include the following:

- A title that describes the volunteer's responsibilities

- The position's importance to the school and the benefits the volunteer gains from the experience (this is an important, yet seldom used, part of a job description)

- The qualifications needed to successfully do the job

- The person(s) to whom the volunteer is responsible

- Detailed descriptions of the volunteer's tasks

- How a volunteer will be trained to prepare for an assignment

- The length of time required for the position, including how many hours per week and the length of the time commitment needed

Recruit Volunteers

Recruitment is the next, and often most challenging, step in the process. Techniques for involving people in volunteer work should be creative and far-reaching. Recruitment should take place throughout the year to replace volunteers as well as to enlist additional assistance for new programs. Two important recruiting issues must be immediately addressed: determining who could be a volunteer and finding ways to reach out and find volunteers.

IDENTIFYING POTENTIAL VOLUNTEERS. Schools and PTAs have depended too long on stay-at-home mothers as their primary source of volunteers. There is, however, a vast, largely untapped reservoir of talent and potential in parents who work full-time. Too often, schools perceive parents' full-time employment as an insurmountable barrier to volunteering. There are, however, creative ways to overcome this barrier. For example, schools often overlook the large population of adults who work second and third shifts—which are predominantly evening hours, weekends, or flexible schedules—as potential daytime volunteers. Parents who work a traditional 9-to-5 schedule may be able to volunteer their time in the evenings, on weekends, or at home (White-Clark, Decker, & Mott, 1996).

Teachers and administrators should be encouraged to consider the range of skills available from parents who work in hospitals, fire and police departments, television and radio stations, and so forth. Parents who work in the evenings for computer services, newspapers, and restaurants are good prospective afternoon volunteers. Adults who work on the weekends in places such as parks, museums, libraries, and churches possess a wealth of talents to contribute to schools, and usually have one or two full days off during the week. Self-employed adults, such as consultants, artists, or musicians, may have flexible schedules that can accommodate volunteering in the daytime or evening.

Senior citizens are another underused, yet highly talented, pool of potential volunteers with skills that are easily adapted to school curriculum and programs. Furthermore, senior volunteers can provide meaningful interactions that increase understanding between and appreciation for other generations. Another important reason to involve senior citizens is their political clout; they make up the highest percentage of registered voters. Effective intergenerational programs can be instrumental in establishing strong alliances with older voters, who then may be more likely to vote on behalf of education advocacy issues and legislation for children.

FINDING PEOPLE TO VOLUNTEER. Instead of waiting for people to volunteer, go out into the community and actively recruit them. Consider arranging meetings at local work sites, senior centers, or retirement communities. At these meetings, volunteer coordinators or teams can talk with prospective candidates about the importance of and the need for their involvement with the school. Other methods of delivering this message can include

- Posters, pamphlets/fliers, and brochures posted or given out at community supermarkets, banks, and/or churches

- Notices in community newsletters or bulletin boards, newspapers, bills, bank statements, payroll checks, and/or coupon booklets

- Booths or exhibits at local stores, malls, and/or community fairs

VOLUNTEERING

Train and Orient Volunteers

The training and orientation of new volunteers is crucial. Effective training can ease anxiety and confusion, alleviate fears, and increase the chances that volunteers will maintain a long-term relationship with the school. Orientation and training sessions should be held at varying times to accommodate everyone's schedules. These sessions should set a welcoming tone and create support for volunteers. They should be relevant, hands-on, and geared toward the specific skills and responsibilities of each volunteer. The supervising teachers or staff should give input into or be a part of the training session along with the PTA coordinator or team. Orientation sessions should familiarize volunteers with the following:

- **SCHOOL FACILITIES.** Provide a map and tour of the building and grounds. Point out important places such as restrooms, the lounge, and the coatroom.

- **SCHOOL STAFF AND TEACHERS.** Introduce volunteers to the principal, teachers, and office and custodial staff. Schedule individual visits with the staff members or teachers with whom the volunteers will work to discuss specific responsibilities and scheduling.

- **SCHOOL PHILOSOPHY AND PROCEDURES.** Provide a job description and a handbook for each volunteer. The handbook should include the school's philosophy and mission, a description of the volunteer program, and the school's operating policies and procedures. It should also include information on confidentiality, ethics for working with students and staff, student discipline, dependability, attendance, and recording volunteer hours. During orientation, provide a time for volunteers to ask questions, discuss information, and fill out forms.

Retain and Recognize Volunteers

While volunteers may choose to become involved for many reasons, their continued commitment and motivation will come from a deeper kind of gratification. To develop and sustain a feeling of belonging and satisfaction among volunteers, it is important that you:

- Provide ongoing training to develop skills that allow volunteers to try new assignments and work with new people

- Train continually, and monitor teachers and staff to ensure that they are effectively working with volunteers

- Treat volunteers like colleagues

- Provide regular activities that recognize volunteers for their work and demonstrate the school's appreciation for their efforts

This recognition needs to be both personal and universal. Each volunteer should be regularly and sincerely acknowledged in ways that he or she feels is appropriate and rewarding. The more the staff knows about their volunteers, the easier it will be to provide this kind of personal recognition. All volunteers should feel a sense of camaraderie and should be honored as a group during specific special events throughout the school year.

A WORD ABOUT SECURITY

Before any volunteer begins service at a school, the school staff should run a routine background check, just as they would for a new staff member. PTAs can also use state police programs to run potential volunteers' names through a database that will notify them of any child sex offense convictions.

Evaluate Volunteer Performance and Program Success

As with any successful program, a volunteer program should be continually evaluated and improved. Surveys, questionnaires, observations, and personal interviews can assess the program's general success in meeting the needs of children, teachers, staff, and volunteers. These methods can also be used to assess the individual performance of each volunteer, the effectiveness of orientation and training sessions, and the volunteer program's procedures and recruitment strategies.

VOLUNTEERING

PROJECT IDEAS

Ideas for PTAs and the School Community Working Together

CLIMATE CONTROL BOX. Place a box near the front office, in which parents can anonymously drop observations and suggestions regarding school climate. Use this information to make the school's climate more inviting to potential volunteers.

HARD-TO-REACH PARENTS. Reach out to parents through routine phone calls or e-mail messages. At open houses or parent nights, the principal and teachers can discuss the goals for the school year with parents. Have each parent complete a card that lists one thing he or she commits to do to help either the teacher or the principal achieve their goals that year. Another idea is to create a bulletin board for parents that highlights home-school projects and volunteer opportunities. Place the board in the entryways of local banks, grocery stores, and so forth, so all parents are informed about school functions and asked to be involved. The board can also provide the school's phone number, so parents can call to get more information, leave ideas or messages, or volunteer their services to staff.

LET YOUR FINGERS DO THE WALKING. Publish a volunteer "yellow pages." Survey parents, seniors citizens, and other community members on their interests, and use the resource book to help match school needs with volunteer talents. List volunteers' names, interests and talents, phone numbers, days and times available, how frequently they would like to participate (including the option of just one time per year), and where they would like to volunteer (at school or from home). Distribute the directory to PTA leaders, principals, teachers, and office staff.

CREATIVE CONTRIBUTIONS. Create volunteer opportunities that go beyond the tasks volunteers traditionally perform. Possibilities might include assisting the school nurse, organizing a letter-writing campaign to focus attention on an education issue, helping develop a drug and alcohol prevention program, teaching mini-courses on subjects such as using computers, organizing parent events, forming fathers' clubs, assisting in special education classes, and providing transportation or child care so another parent can volunteer.

HOW CAN WE EVER THANK YOU? Show appreciation for volunteers by creating a wall of fame display, with pictures of volunteers helping with school activities and events. Publicize the contributions of volunteers in school newsletters, and provide incentives for volunteering. These incentives could include awards or certificates to honor volunteers or coupons indicating their number of volunteer hours, which can be used at a "volunteer store" to purchase donated materials and gifts.

SENIOR POWER. Send out surveys to local retirement communities or senior clubs to find seniors interested in volunteering in schools. There are a variety of ways seniors can volunteer. They might share their life experiences when those experiences relate to classroom topics. For example, a survivor of the Holocaust might talk to a history class, or a retired carpenter might assist in a wood shop class. Seniors might also assist teachers on a weekly basis with classroom duties, or be cast in school plays.

Ideas for Working Parents

WEEKEND AND EVENING COORDINATORS. Have parents supervise and coordinate weekend or evening activities at the school, such as sports events, spelling bees, and homework assistance programs. Parents who would otherwise need child-care help to volunteer may be able to bring their younger children to these activities.

CONSULTING THE EXPERTS. Consult school staff and parents on their areas of expertise, and have them speak to students about their careers, the kinds of skills used in their jobs, and the education or training they need to do their jobs. Have parents who work in public relations, advertising, or marketing arrange publicity for a school program, take pictures or videos of students, and develop media presentations for school use.

Ideas for Teachers

WE'RE LOOKING FOR A FEW GOOD VOLUNTEERS. Teachers can recruit volunteers by sending home a monthly calendar that helps parents plan ahead and sign up for specific days to volunteer. Another way to recruit volunteers is to ask children to invite their parents to participate in classroom projects and school events. Teachers should provide specific volunteer activities for parents when they come into the classroom.

"LET ME GIVE YOU MY CARD . . ." Print business cards for teachers that include their names, subjects they teach, phone numbers, and best times to call. On the back, list ways parents could assist in the classroom. Teachers can distribute these to parents at back-to-school nights.

CULTURAL AWARENESS MONTHS. Designate cultural awareness months at your school to celebrate the diverse cultures represented in your community. Ask parents from all backgrounds to become involved in cultural events by speaking to classes about their family's and their culture's customs and traditions, foods, dances, and arts and crafts.

Ideas for PTAs Working With Middle and High School Communities

While middle and high school students are more reluctant to have a parent directly involved in their classrooms, research has shown the positive effects of some type of parent involvement at these levels as well (Henderson & Berla, 1995).

HIKING IN THE HALLS. Consider a program that encourages parents to get their exercise by walking at the high school instead of at a health or fitness club. After picking up a volunteer badge at the office, these parents perform an important service by increasing the adult presence in the building and thereby reducing behavior problems. Parents can also become better acquainted with the school and with their children's friends and teachers.

CALLING ALL EXPERTS. Create a program that has alumni, parents, or community members contributing to the curriculum on a regular basis. For example, volunteers could enrich social studies units and history classes by speaking on topics about which they have personal experience, such as World War II or the Civil Rights movement. In geography, history, or foreign language classes, encourage adults who have traveled, been in the military, come from other countries, or who speak foreign languages to share their personal experiences, the history of other countries, and photographs or slides. Ask volunteers with appropriate expertise to assist in vocational classrooms or laboratories such as shop, auto mechanics, or consumer education.

ENTREPRENEURSHIP 101. Invite adults who have business backgrounds to team up with teachers to create yearlong classroom projects that focus on developing student-operated businesses. Parents can help teachers instruct students on how to conduct market research to determine product lines and on how to produce and sell the product in the community. They can also actively assist students in negotiating financing for their businesses from local banks and businesses.

ADOPT-A-PROGRAM. Allow volunteers to adopt and sponsor an academic program, a school club, or a school team, and to support it throughout the school year. For example, parents could assist the staff and students with the publication of the yearbook, newspaper, or literary magazine.

PEER MENTORS. Volunteers can serve as peer mentors for parents having difficulty with their children. These mentors can advise and comfort other parents and can share strategies that have helped them resolve similar problems. Mentors can attend a training course developed by a parent involvement professional or a professional counselor from the community.

BEST PRACTICES

Each community and each set of volunteers are unique. These programs should be considered as guidelines. If you think a program might work for you, adapt it to your situation.

Excel City

Berkman Elementary School is a bilingual accelerated Title I school in Round Rock, Texas. More than half of Berkman's students are from minority groups and 71% of them are eligible for a free or reduced lunch. The majority of students are also from single-parent homes. At Berkman, teachers, parents, businesspeople, and students work together to create Excel City, a student-run model city that has its own businesses, government, and monetary systems. Excel City employees, employers, and elected officials are all fifth graders. The rest of the student body—from preschoolers to fifth graders—are the city's consumers and citizens.

Round Rock businesses, service organizations, and parents have donated almost all of the equipment and materials needed for Excel City. The school raises any necessary extra funds through a variety of sources, such as a student-run convenience store, student bake sales and car washes, arts and crafts sales, and awards and grants.

Just like a real town, Excel City has a bank, a postal system, a thrift store, a convenience store, an arts-and-crafts store, a publishing company, a garden center, a recycling center, and a newspaper. Play money to spend at these stores is earned by students for good conduct, academic achievement, good attendance, and for selling pieces of writing to the Excel City's publishing company.

To make Excel City work, Berkman School teachers and staff received training in the Accelerated Schools Process, which was developed by Harry Levin at Stanford University. Parents help train students for work in Excel City, and also oversee Excel City elections, observe student activities within the model city, take students on field trips to Round Rock businesses, and help with fund-raising. Because of the project, a record number of parents have become involved in Berkman's PTA and in planning the school's future.

Respect Yourself

At Evergreen Junior High School in Evergreen, Colorado, students learn about life issues from parents through a program called Respect.

With the help of the Evergreen Junior High PTA, parent volunteers meet monthly with about 30 students in a focus group to discuss topics pertinent to their lives—such as harassment, bullying, discrimination, ethics, music, relationships, goal setting, and student self-respect—with an emphasis on making positive personal choices.

The curriculum emphasizes student-led meetings, small discussion groups, and interactive activities such as role-playing to increase the sharing of ideas. Most parents do not teach their own children's classes. Classes are held early in the day to allow many working parents and community leaders to participate.

Parents in the Halls

Overcrowding at Mandarin Middle School in Jacksonville, Florida, has parents participating in a program that teaches them to be hall monitors. The Hall Monitor Program addresses safety concerns due to overcrowding in the hallways, student concerns about locating classes or offices, and concerns about school security. As hall monitors, parents also become comfortable and familiar with the school.

Parent hall monitors work in teams of two. Each member of the team keeps in touch with the other team member through walkie-talkies and whistles. Monitors circulate through the school bus areas, school hallways, and grounds watching for disruptions, answering questions, and directing parents and other visitors. Volunteer monitors receive a booklet with basic instructions on how to handle out-of-control situations, a map of the school building, class schedules, a list of frequently asked questions, and a green golf shirt "uniform" to make them easier to see in the halls.

The PTA holds several training classes per year for the program in cooperation with school administration, staff, and a police officer. Parents are invited to sign up for the program during school orientations, open houses, volunteer orientations, and on volunteer resource sheets. They are encouraged to sign up for specific times and days, and many parents choose to volunteer before they go to work or during their lunch hour. If a parent's schedule does not allow him or her to dedicate a specific time, the parent is encouraged to come as time permits. Parents of incoming sixth graders are especially encouraged to become hall monitors. This can help students make smoother transitions from elementary school to middle school.

Parents Making a Difference

More than 200 parents volunteer at Tomasita Elementary School in Albuquerque, New Mexico, in a variety of school programs. This number is remarkable because the total enrollment for the school is only 475.

Parent volunteers completely run the school's free preschool program. Through a foster grandparents program, older volunteers help in classrooms, work with children on assignments, play games to reinforce skills, and read to them. Parents, middle school students, and high school students tutor elementary students after school twice a week.

Tomasita also receives a tremendous amount of help from volunteers in other ways. School staff and educators, families, and community businesses donate food to families in need. And the school's Clothing Bank gives secondhand clothing items to students and their families. A team of teachers and parents also meet monthly to plan the instructional focus and support activities for the school.

Paideia Program

Parents are required to volunteer 18 hours each year and attend two parent-teacher conferences at a public K–12 magnet school in Chattanooga, Tennessee, called the Chattanooga School for the Arts and Sciences (CSAS).

CSAS follows the Paideia (pronounced Pie-dee-ah) model for education, and CSAS educators believe that parent involvement is vital in developing students' love of learning. At CSAS, all parents are expected to assist in the classroom, help with field trips, teach mini-courses for parents, or take part in the Parent-Teacher-Student Association. Parents are also active in advisory groups and attend sessions about teaching methods used in the school and books and materials to be used in classes. Furthermore, parents help clean and fix up the school on Saturdays.

Teachers contribute by keeping in close contact with parents and giving parents ideas on how they can assist in their children's education through home activities.

No extra funds are needed for parent involvement, but the payoffs are high. The school has a 96% attendance rate, which is higher than that of other Hamilton County Schools, and 95% of CSAS graduates go to college.

Senior Help

Parents of students at Pleasantview Elementary School in Franklin, Wisconsin, may not always be able to volunteer during the school day, but the community's senior citizens often can be found helping out instead.

A group of senior citizens comes to the school's library each week to read to children and provide one-on-one reading assistance for children who need extra help. The seniors often have lunch at the school with the children, and twice a year the school offers an appreciation breakfast to its senior volunteers.

CHAPTER 6

STANDARD V: SCHOOL DECISION MAKING AND ADVOCACY

*Definition: Parents are full partners in decisions
that affect children and families.*

ALTHOUGH THEY MAY NOT REALIZE IT, most parents probably already have taken the first steps to being effective advocates for their children. Every time parents stand up for their children or look for ways to improve their children's school experience, they are acting as advocates. As such, they have an effect, however subtle, on the decision-making process. When parents link up with other parents who have similar objectives, or when parents speak for children other than their own, they take the role of advocate to another level—working for the good of many.

In the advocate/decision-maker role, parents work with the school to help solve problems and develop policies that make the school system more responsive and equitable to all families. Standard V places this effort at the center of a parent's engagement in the child's education. Committing to this standard can lead to the highest level of parent involvement in education, with benefits on all sides—the parent, the school, and the child.

ADVOCACY

This chapter offers effective ways for parents to advocate for children on school- and education-related issues and to be part of the decision-making process at school. For example, by volunteering at school, tutoring at home, and communicating at parent-teacher conferences, parents can learn more about the school's structure and programs. The more experience parents gain in working with school staff and educators, the more effective they will be in their advocacy role.

Parents can fulfill the decision-making role at school by serving on advisory committees, education standards and assessment design teams, and site-based management teams and by participating in other kinds of advocacy and decision-making activities. As with the other parenting roles, results come more quickly and easily when families are prepared and supported by the school's staff and educators.

Parent volunteer June Cavarretta, a member of a school improvement team in Carpentersville, Illinois, says of advocacy: "My work counts. My voice is heard. I've made a difference for my children" (Cavarretta, 1998, p. 15).

PARENTS AS ADVOCATES

Any action parents take to improve the lives of children, whether in their communities or at the state and federal level, is advocacy. Parents can be advocates in many different ways. For example, once an issue affecting children has been identified, parents can research the issue, disseminate information to other concerned people, raise questions for discussion at local schools or town meetings, propose potential solutions or remedies, provide updates on the status of the issue, train other advocates, and otherwise involve people in the effort and activities.

When organized and united, parents can be a powerful voice on behalf of their children. Effective advocacy, however, requires that parents develop a plan that includes a strong message and a strategy for communicating that message to people such as lawmakers, the media, and community members. The plan should outline how to recruit other participants, train them, and keep them motivated through what may be a long and arduous effort. A well-developed plan allows advocates to focus their energy on activities that will improve children's and families' lives.

HEAD START—
A PARENTAL ADVOCACY SUCCESS STORY

When the continued survival of Head Start Programs was threatened during the Nixon administration, parents and administrators realized that they had to act together to defend this program that had helped so many children achieve educational and personal success. Determined to protect the welfare of the Head Start constituency—poor children from birth to 5 years old and their families—Head Start program directors, parents, and staff joined to form the National Head Start Association in 1973. The organization's goal was to defend Head Start in Congress. Not only was the program saved, but the new structure of the Head Start organization caused the program to flourish. Today it represents 2,051 Head Start programs in the United States, improving the lives of 750,000 children.

The involvement of parents has been critical to Head Start's success. Parent Committees at Head Start schools give parents of enrolled children the opportunity to assist in the adoption of policies that address their interests and needs and support the education and healthy development of their children. Local Head Start agencies provide parents, community representatives, community partners, and staff with training on program governance and shared decision making, so they can understand and support the purpose of the local Head Start policy-making agency (a policy council or committee) and the Parent Committee. The creation of detailed guidelines and informational materials have greatly contributed to the continuing accomplishments of Head Start programs. While the Head Start charter is specifically targeted to support at-risk children and their families, the same principles of organization and cooperation that saved Head Start can bring many of the same benefits to a broader student population.

ADVOCACY

SITE-BASED MANAGEMENT TEAMS

Cooperative structures that involve parents in decision making may be called many things. Head Start has a policy council; other organizations may create a steering committee or a parents' advisory committee. These groups are different types of *site-based management teams.*

Site-based management is a method of addressing school operations and policy decisions through a group or committee composed of parents, educators, administrators, and even students—with all constituencies present in varying proportions. In many instances, smaller, task force–type committees address specific issues, then report to and have ongoing, open dialogue with a larger site-based management team.

By the early 1990s, approximately one third of all school districts had some version of site-based management (Ogawa & White, 1994, p. 55). By 1993, 44 states practiced site-based management in some school districts, and states such as Kentucky and Texas required statewide site-based management (Leithwood & Menzies, 1998, p. 325). All states now either permit or require site-based management (*Education Week,* 1999, p. 119).

In 1998, researchers Kenneth Leithwood from the Ontario Institute for Studies in Education and Teresa Menzies from Brock University in Ontario examined 83 studies of site-based management in U.S. schools and found that it can take many forms. Although all forms of site-based management involve parents in some way, the amount of power and authority shared with them varies greatly. Leithwood and Menzies' examination revealed four basic forms of site-based management teams.

1. Parents are informed, but principals retain authority. This form does the least to effect school change.

2. Some teachers exercise control. This form has the greatest positive impact on teachers.

3. Parents and the community are in charge. This form brings about the most changes, but some of the changes are negative.

4. Parents, community members, teachers, and administrators share decision-making power. This last form emulates the Japanese business principle, which shifts emphasis away from a single person in authority and places it on the contributions of all to manage and practice team leadership. Because this form is the least practiced, there is little research to document its effects (Leithwood & Menzies, 1998).

RESEARCH FINDINGS

Research has documented that parent involvement in school decision making—through site-based management teams or other formalized structures—can provide many benefits to all parties, including the following (Epstein et al., 1997):

Students

- Understand that their rights are protected

- Become more aware of families' representation in school decisions

- Benefit from specific policies enacted by parent/school committees

Parents

- Gain a voice in school decisions and policies that affect children

- Become aware of school and district policies

- Feel a sense of ownership in their children's school

Teachers and Administrators

- Become aware of the contributions parents can make to school policy development and decisions

- Grow to accept the equality of parents serving on school committees

Despite these research findings and the fact that many states have laws providing for parent involvement based on federal Title I provisions,

ADVOCACY

the number of school administrations that *equally* share the decision-making process with parents, teachers, and the community remains small. This role requires a concerted effort on the part of educators to ensure parents are valued in this role. Paying attention to the scheduling of meetings, language used in meetings, and ratio of parents to staff are all critical. Ongoing training is essential.

THE ROLE OF PARENTS IN SCHOOL DECISION MAKING AND ITS EFFECTS ON SCHOOLS

The appropriate role of parents in school-related decisions has been the subject of much debate. Many supporters feel that parent involvement in discussions and decisions about school operations, education standards, and school accountability is a fundamental part of school reform. These proponents also believe that until a presidential or congressional commission is appointed to evaluate and encourage effective parent involvement in school governance at a national level, real improvements in schools will not take place (Lewis & Henderson, 1997; Sarason, 1995).

There are many ways for parents to become advocates, advisors, and decision makers. They can become active in school decision making by attending meetings regularly, sharing their opinions on school-related issues with educators, and exercising their right to participate as partners in the decision-making process concerning programs and other decisions that affect their children. Parents can also become involved in school issues by running for election to the school board or a school council committee, volunteering to serve on a PTA legislative committee, or serving on a school task force. Parents on these committees can, in turn, help keep other parents informed about specific issues and laws that affect their children's schools.

Educators can do much to help parents become involved at this level. Educators can share with parents their insights into the process of education, school operations, child development, and diversity issues. Educators can encourage parents to participate in school-related decisions by encouraging them to serve on advisory councils/committees that are responsible for addressing everything from curriculum development and textbook selection, to disciplinary policies and dress codes.

With the additional help and support of administrators and school board members, parents can add meaningful perspectives to committees that interview and hire school staff.

Effectively Involving Parents in School Decisions

AT THE LOCAL LEVEL. For parents to effectively advocate and negotiate for all children in a school setting, there must be a forum in which this type of activity can occur. Some schools create site-based management teams, others form school governance councils, and still others create a variety of advisory committees. PTAs can educate parents on how to be an advocate for all children in the school and on how to serve as members of site-based management teams or other school committees. Whatever structure a school adopts, success can be ensured only when all participants must do their part at all levels of the education system.

Effective local advisory committees include members of different genders, roles, and ethnic backgrounds. It is essential that these diverse members work together to write a clear vision statement that includes a defined set of goals and bylaws that define the limitation of the group's power. The group should elect a chairperson who possesses the skills to lead and empower each team member. The chairperson does not have to be the school principal, although for any local advisory committee to be successful, it must have the principal's support and guidance. Whatever role the principal assumes within the group, he or she should make it a priority to empower others and create conditions for everyone to work together to attain common goals.

AT THE DISTRICT LEVEL. To facilitate parent involvement, a school district needs to create a policy that specifies the relationship between itself and the local advisory committees. District officials, for example, may find it valuable to retain people at the district level to serve as consultants or technical assistants to the local advisory committee members. In its new relationship with local advisory committees, the district needs to maintain open communication with local schools. PTAs can facilitate this type of communication by involving themselves in school district committees and task forces. PTAs should ensure that parents serve on district-level site-based management teams and should then

ADVOCACY

inform local advisory committees about the progress of these groups. Working with principals, PTAs can use newsletters, bulletins, public forums, and parent education nights to inform parents and community members about the issues facing their district.

AT THE STATE LEVEL. As state legislators consider, draft, and vote on legislation that provides for parent involvement in schools, the voices of parents, teachers, and school administrators must be heard and included in the debate. PTA members can become involved in statewide issues by writing, calling, or visiting their legislators to voice their support of or opposition to proposed legislation.

AT THE NATIONAL LEVEL. Most parents focus their advocacy efforts on the local or state level, but parents can also influence policy at the federal level. Federal advocacy efforts may be directed toward the U.S. Congress, which makes the law, and the president and federal administrative agencies, which implement and enforce the law. As these leaders draft and vote on education legislation, the voices of parents, teachers, and school administrators must be heard and included in the discussion. There are many times during the federal legislative and regulatory process when parents may seek to influence policy. For example, parents may contact their congressional representatives to express their support of or opposition to any bill and make alternative suggestions. They may bolster their own opinions by engaging in petition drives or letter-writing campaigns and delivering the results to their congressional representatives. They may ask to appear as witnesses or submit written testimony to committees seeking information on an issue of interest. Parents can contact members of the U.S. Congress by accessing their websites at www.senate.gov or www.house.gov. Parents can also call the national switchboard at (202) 224-3121.

In addition, advocates may contact and urge the president to sign or veto a bill. Even after a bill has been made into law, the public has the opportunity to comment on proposed regulations that will serve as guidelines for administering the law. Interested parties may also submit a written statement in support of or opposition to legal challenges, should a law or regulation be challenged in court.

BARRIERS TO EFFECTIVE PARENT INVOLVEMENT IN SCHOOL DECISION MAKING

According to national surveys, although most parents want to play a more active role in decision making, most teachers and administrators are often reluctant to support this type of involvement (Lewis & Henderson, 1997). The complex reasons for this reluctance are discussed briefly below.

Labeling

One of the most pervasive barriers is the tendency to make assumptions about, or label, people based on a group they belong to. Labeling—the assignment of personality characteristics based on appearance or superficial behaviors—is a normal process inherent to human nature. However, labeling can become negative when it is used to describe people's deficits rather than their assets. When one thinks of labels for such groups as teens, teachers, or parents, a variety of adjectives comes to mind. Not all of them are positive. Negative labels can be even more charged when these groups' roles in decision making are considered. For the benefit of the school district and every child in it, site-based management team members must learn to view others in terms of their real strengths and assets, rather than in terms of unfair and inaccurate labels.

Other barriers that have nothing to do with team composition or conduct can also interfere with productive and successful site-based management teams. The following section examines the barriers that professional boundaries can contribute to this problem.

Professional Boundaries

Educators and administrators often believe that their training establishes a boundary—it gives them a set of responsibilities and domains that are theirs alone. Some believe that this "boundary" between professional educator and parent protects students and schools by preserving the power and authority gained through formal training and experience. While the expertise of administrators and educators is critical to providing a healthy school environment, parent involvement should not be seen as a threat to that authority. Barriers involving boundaries are explored in more depth in Richard Neal's 1991 book, *School-Based Management: A Detailed Guide for Successful Implementation,* and Seymour Sarason's 1995 book, *Parent Involvement and the Political Principle: Why the Existing Governance Structure of Schools Should Be Abolished.*

BARRIERS FOR TEACHERS. Teachers face two kinds of barriers. First, because teachers traditionally have been independent in teaching and running their classrooms, they do not always know how to welcome and work with others in their domain. Second, because some teachers belong to unions, site-based management team decisions that affect time requirements, class size, and ancillary duties may conflict with collective bargaining agreements. For example, a policy generated by a site-based management team may call for before- and after-school activities that would require the school to operate beyond its normal hours. If teachers are willing to serve in this capacity, their union contract may have to be renegotiated to accommodate these additional hours.

BARRIERS FOR PTA LEADERS AND MEMBERS. Parents actively involved in the PTA may be perceived by administrators as insiders who are interested in school matters. Therefore, they often are the ones invited to serve on site-based management teams. On the other hand, parents who are not involved in the PTA may be wrongly identified as outsiders who are not interested in school policies. If so, they may not feel welcome to serve. One of the goals of all site-based management systems should be to make all parents feel that their talents and insights are welcome.

BARRIERS FOR PRINCIPALS. Principals are usually considered the chief decision makers in school settings. Therefore, they may see site-based management as a threat to their authority, which is already shared with and limited by superintendents and the school board.

BARRIERS FOR SUPERINTENDENTS. Superintendents tend to be strong, decisive individuals who place a premium on how efficiently tasks can be accomplished. As such, they may be reluctant to share authority. Superintendents and principals need to realize that site-based management can provide a way for them to delegate and share responsibility for getting things done. When done properly, site-based management can actually enhance the power of superintendents and principals to become more effective in the district or school they serve.

BARRIERS FOR SCHOOL BOARDS. For a site-based management program to work, it must be supported by the school board. Some boards may be reluctant to do this because they fear that decentralizing management will lead to problems with focus and responsibility. For example, if each school is allowed to be different in terms of its decision-making practices, and decisions by the board no longer affect all schools, how can the board ensure fairness? School boards must be assured that there are ways to support parent involvement while maintaining the board's legitimate responsibilities.

This can be established in the planning process of making the transition to a decentralized management system. School boards can identify what issues will be handled by the board and what matters will be left to the discretion of the local schools. For example, a board may decide that the food service program will continue to be directed by the central office, while delegating the purchasing of school supplies and equipment to the local schools. Boards can then begin to act in more of a consulting role rather than a directing one.

BARRIERS FOR PARENTS. Parents and others who make the effort to become involved in school decisions can themselves become barriers to successful site-based management. Teams are only as good as their members. If site-based management team members fall into the trap of focusing on inter-team politics, personalities, and egos, then the team is destined to fail. The process will become frustrating, and team members will help neither themselves nor the children. Perhaps even more significant, such failures provide ammunition to opponents who wish to end or prevent the use of site-based management at their schools.

BREAKING DOWN THE BARRIERS

Professional boundaries and labels, as well as other barriers—such as lack of time, planning, and money—inhibit the development of genuine trust and respect among parents, teachers, and administrators.

Open and honest communication is the key to surmounting these barriers. Communication is a necessary component in establishing site-based management teams that are based on mutual trust and respect. It allows PTA leaders, parents, teachers, and administrators to contribute to decisions that affect children. Those involved in the process must overcome their reluctance to listen to views that differ from their own. They must also be willing to listen to the views of people with less or more status than they have, and of those whose experience may not seem immediately relevant enough to merit their participation in the process.

Effective partnerships develop when each partner is respected and empowered to fully participate in the decision-making process. Parents and educators must depend on shared authority in the decision-making process to foster trust and mutual support of each other's efforts to help students succeed. It is crucial to involve parents, either as individuals or as representatives of others, in collaborative decision-making processes on issues from curriculum and course selection to discipline policies and overall school reform measures.

Breaking Down Barriers at the Local Level

PTAs have traditionally given parents and teachers an opportunity to work together. These associations have provided parents a collective voice in decisions on volunteering and planning school/PTA programs. By working with teachers and administrators to establish site-based management teams or other, smaller committees that give parents a voice in school governance, PTAs can be a powerful factor in taking parents' involvement in decision making to a higher level. In creating effective site-based management teams, PTA leaders should work with administrators and teachers to implement the suggestions in the "Quality Tips for Successful Programs" section beginning on the next page.

Breaking Down Barriers at Higher Levels

Unfortunately, there may be situations in which a school's superintendent does not support site-based management or any form of parent involvement. As a result, other educators, such as teachers and principals, may hesitate to become involved. If this happens, parents can turn to the school district's governing authority—the school board. While this process is necessarily delicate, involving issues of ego and authority, it should not be deferred. When the situation requires a direct appeal to the school board, parents can take the following steps:

- Attend a school board meeting with a small group of parents who support site-based management. At the meeting, have one person from the group briefly state the case for parent involvement.

- Supply school board members with information supporting the group's views.

- Give school board members a petition signed by local voters who support parent involvement.

More suggestions on overcoming barriers and working to build partnerships are provided in chapter 8.

QUALITY TIPS FOR SUCCESSFUL PROGRAMS

The key to establishing a successful parent involvement program is to create an environment of openness and trust. For better or worse, this responsibility falls largely on the shoulders of school administrators and teachers who are the insiders when it comes to policy decisions and operations. Because of this, most of the tips below are directed at what administrators and teachers can do to involve parents in the decision-making process. Some tips can be implemented by any group member, including parents.

Providing Knowledge/Training

- Treat parents' concerns with respect, and demonstrate genuine interest in developing solutions.

- Include parents on all decision-making and advisory committees, and offer understandable, accessible, and well-publicized ways to influence decisions, raise issues or concerns, appeal decisions, and resolve problems within such committees.

ADVOCACY

- Offer training for staff and parents on collaborative partnering, group problem solving, team building, conflict resolution, time management, and shared decision making.

Sharing Information

- Use the parents' native language to provide them with current information on school policies, practices, and student and school performance data.

- Promote communication and provide up-to-date information on current issues by establishing interactive computer systems that electronically link school sites with the district office.

- Publish results of surveys that assess educators' or community members' satisfaction with the site-based management team's work.

Taking Action

- Form PTAs to help parents identify and respond to issues.

- Encourage active parent participation in the decisions that affect students, such as student placement, course selection, and individual personalized education plans.

- Promote parent participation on school district, state, and national committees and issues.

Rewarding Participants

- Recognize the efforts of the principal, educators, and parents on site-based management teams through thank-you notes, public acknowledgments in newsletters, or recognition at faculty meetings.

- Schedule year-round functions, formal dinners, and award presentations to celebrate the site-based management team's achievements.

PROJECT IDEAS

Ideas for PTAs and the School Community Working Together

PARENT INVOLVEMENT POLICY. Work with students, parents, teachers, school administrators, community leaders, and businesspeople to develop a policy that establishes the vision, common mission, and foundation for parent/family involvement programs in your community. (See chapter 9 for information on how to develop a parent involvement policy.)

PARENT INVOLVEMENT MONTH. Plan a parent involvement month that includes the following activities:

- In cooperation with school administrators, sponsor a series of town meetings where school officials describe school programs and services and share annual reports containing performance data. Following these presentations, parents, staff, and community members can discuss the information presented by school officials and make suggestions for future goals.

- Interview parents at these events, and publish their opinions on the issues and the outcomes of the meetings in school newsletters, local papers, and on the school's website. Publish any successful changes in school or program operations that are the result of parent initiation and involvement.

- Sponsor an advocate training program where parents learn how to effectively advocate for their children in school situations such as parent-teacher conferences, school board meetings, and other public forums where decisions that affect children are being made. As an annual tradition, this can become a process for continuous improvement.

"AS YOUR PARENT REPRESENTATIVE, I PROMISE TO . . ." If school policy permits, hold elections to facilitate parent participation on school committees or other community groups that are involved in policy and program decisions. Advertise committee assignments well in advance and actively recruit representatives. Elected parents should receive clear program goals and objectives, monitor the steps taken to reach program

ADVOCACY

goals, and be able to help other parents understand program expectations and changes.

CONVENING FOR BETTER PARENT INVOLVEMENT. Work to bring administrators and PTA members together by sending school officials to the annual state PTA convention. This can be financed either by allocating money in the school budget or by seeking business donations. At the convention, school officials can learn about the PTA's mission, how to work more effectively with local PTAs, the benefits of adding parent involvement activities to the job descriptions for principals and teachers, and how to encourage school administrators to attend PTA meetings.

ASSESSMENT FORUM FOR PARENTS. Hold an interactive forum to discuss the school's education standards, the assessment and testing process, school expectations, and how parents can help at home to support the standards being taught at the school. Present the information in easy-to-understand language, and provide each parent with a parent handbook that describes the material covered in the forum.

Ideas for Teachers

CLASSROOM COMMITTEE. Form a classroom committee, and hold evening meetings at school or in parents' homes. During these meetings, you can create or discuss with parents the classroom's daily routine, the academic plans and goals for the school year, the classroom's discipline and homework policies, and the school's assessment and grading procedures. These committees can also be used to plan classroom field trips and special projects.

YOUR OPINION COUNTS! Include a short survey in classroom newsletters that asks parents for their input on lessons, activities, and field trips described in the newsletter.

PARENT PARTNERS FOR PROGRESS. Form problem-solving partnerships with parents to discuss concerns about their children. Get parents' input on their children's habits, behaviors, and moods at home. Express confidence in your ability to solve the problems together, devise a plan of action that will be implemented at home and at school, and make plans to meet again to discuss the child's progress.

Ideas for PTAs Working With Middle and High School Communities

ADVOCACY GUIDE. Encourage the development of a planning and advocacy handbook for parents on students' rights and responsibilities. This handbook will help inform parents and students about the school's rules, consequences for breaking rules, and how parents can appeal if they do not agree with a school policy.

LEARNING TO LEAD. If school policy permits, promote the idea of electing students to serve on school committees that work on projects related to the curriculum and policy. To promote leadership and advocacy, sponsor a series of workshops in which elected parents and students can receive advocacy training, and ask more experienced parents or student leaders to serve as mentors.

STICKING TOGETHER. Encourage the creation of a greater sense of family in schools by clustering students from a number of classes into smaller units within the school population. To each cluster of students, assign a counselor who can oversee these students throughout their school years. In a similar manner, you may also create teams of teachers that stay with students for more than one year. This will help students form ongoing relationships with adults who understand them and know their strengths and areas that need improvement.

PARENT-TEACHER-ADMINISTRATOR MEDIATION. Support the concept of assigning teachers to act as parent advocates between parents and school administrators in disagreements on behavioral problems and disciplinary actions. Teachers can help bridge gaps of perspective and language, and bring parents and administrators together to focus on the needs of the students.

INFORMATION FOR THE FUTURE. Sponsor seminars to inform high school parents about placement decisions, career planning, and preparation for postsecondary opportunities and how they affect students' future options. For parents who cannot attend, keep them informed through letters, phone calls, e-mail messages, or individual meetings.

ADVOCACY

BEST PRACTICES

Each community and each set of volunteers are unique. These programs should be considered as guidelines. If you think a program might work for you, adapt it to your situation.

Team Effort

Parents have a strong voice in all decisions affecting the Dr. Martin Luther King Elementary and Middle School for Science and Technology in New Orleans, Louisiana. King Elementary is an inner-city school; 99% of its 220 students are African American. The school's main governing body is a 20-member School Planning and Management Team (SPMT). The team includes seven parents, teachers from each grade level, the principal, the assistant principal, community members, and business sponsors.

The school's PTA decides which parents to recommend for the SPMT, basing the recommendations on volunteer hours, knowledge of the community, and personality and leadership qualities that would make someone a good liaison to other parents. A parent must be a PTA member to be on the SPMT.

The SPMT hears all discussions and debate on major school issues and makes all major decisions affecting the school, such as approving the budget and deciding how funds will be spent within the school. All SPMT members are also responsible for establishing a school improvement plan and continually reviewing and revising the plan as needed. All parents can give the team input and feedback through parent meetings and surveys. Furthermore, parents can join subcommittees, which are formed to address specific issues such as discipline, safety, and curriculum.

Beyond Making Photocopies

Parents in Community Unit School District 300 in Carpentersville, Illinois, do more than volunteer in traditional ways. More than 400 parent volunteers in that district have been trained to participate in their children's education through shared decision making.

Several planning teams were created to effect academic reform at the district. Each team focuses on one central issue, such as curriculum or textbook selection. At least half of each team's members are parents and community members. The rest of the members are teachers, students, and administrators.

A planning team works by first creating a mission based on student needs and then setting goals to achieve that mission. All planning team decisions are presented to the board of education for final approval. Continuous training efforts support these teams, and twice each year, team members attend two-week workshops to learn about trust, collaboration, and shared vision.

Under this model, planning teams adopted high school block scheduling, implemented a dress code for one of the middle schools, and started multi-age classrooms and looping (teachers having classes of the same children for several years).

Unleashing PTA Power

In the mid-1990s, the Maine PTA wanted to see a bill called Maine's Learning Results passed into a law. This bill called for all Maine public school graduates to be clear and effective communicators, self-directed, lifelong learners and creative and practical problem solvers, responsible and involved citizens, collaborative and quality workers, and integrative and informed thinkers.

The Maine PTA supported this bill and was awarded a National PTA New Initiatives Grant to conduct advocacy training across the state to inform PTA members and their communities on how to support the bill. The Maine PTA conducted three advocacy training workshops in different parts of the state, flooded its members with information on the bill at its convention, and mobilized support for the bill at the PTA Day at the Capital event. The association also mobilized its member-to-member network, which contacted PTA members across the state, urging them to talk to legislators who were either opposed to or undecided about the bill.

Maine's governor signed the bill into law in June 1997.

ADVOCACY

The Most Powerful Tool: Knowledge

Because knowledge is one of the keys to making good decisions, the Arizona PTA reached out to parents and children in 1997 and 1998 to teach them more about pending legislation. The PTA's reasoning was that this training would give parents the knowledge they needed to make informed decisions at that time, and children would receive a foundation for making good decisions about government later on.

Through a program named KIDS CALL (Concerned About Local Legislation), students from around the state were invited to sign up for a one-day government education event in the state capital. Funding for the program allowed 520 fourth and fifth graders to participate. The National PTA's vice president for legislation and Arizona state officials, including the governor, attorney general, and superintendent of public education, addressed the students. Students then visited four information stations to learn more about the legislative process, and the Arizona League of Women Voters presented a program on how a bill becomes a law. PTA student members gave the children a tour of the capitol, and state legislators met with the children for a question-and-answer session.

Parents learned about legislation during an event called Parents Day at the Legislature, which was sponsored by the Arizona PTA, the Arizona League of Women Voters, and state and community educational organizations. Parents received an overview of current legislative issues involving children and education, underwent advocacy training, and received insight into school funding.

For these programs, the Arizona PTA won the National PTA's Together Everyone Achieves Membership (TEAM) Award in the community outreach category for state PTAs in 1997 and 1998.

Embracing the Nontraditional

Parents and PTA members are actively involved at every level at the Applied Learning Academy, a public middle school in Fort Worth, Texas. The 270 students in grades 6-8 reflect a racial/ethnic balance of 38% Caucasian, 30% African American, 30% Hispanic, and 2% other groups.

Students learn curriculum content as they solve problems or actively work to fulfill important needs at the school or community level.

In 1997 the school adopted the academic standards developed by the Learning Research and Development Center at the University of Pittsburgh and the National Center on Education and the Economy in cooperation with the Fort Worth Independent School District (ISD). The school's new standards assessment system includes three elements:

1. Performance standards built directly on the content standards developed by the national professional organizations for the individual disciplines

2. An on-demand examination

3. A portfolio assessment system

The school's administrators believe that their school's success depends heavily on parents and the community helping to fulfill its goals. Local businesses support the school. Parents can get involved in school decisions by taking part in various teams or committees that evaluate areas in the school such as academic standards, facilities, special events, and so forth. PTA has also worked with the Fort Worth ISD to publish a parent handbook that explains the standards and the assessment process, school expectations, and how parents can help their children at home.

Parents also actively participate in student assessments, which are conducted twice a year in the form of portfolio conferencing. The student presents his or her work portfolio and tells how it meets the academic standards. The teachers provide a written narrative of the student's progress and a checklist of the standards. Together, student, teachers, and parents develop goals for the student for the next academic term.

Learning to Get Involved

Paul Robeson High School in the Englewood area of Chicago, Illinois, opens its doors to any parent willing to get involved. And if parents do not know how to get involved, educators can teach them. Ninety-nine percent of the school's students are African American.

ADVOCACY

The school offers parents a seminar on how to write grant proposals for the school and classes on how to produce a school newsletter by using desktop publishing. Parents also participate in a mentoring program, acting as surrogate parents to students and serving as role models to other parents on how to get involved.

Furthermore, teachers, paraprofessionals, parents, and students serve together on a school-based management team to monitor the school's day-to-day operations, take responsibility for the buildings and grounds activities, and initiate suggestions for school improvement. Parents and teachers may also serve on the Local School Council (LSC), which, as in all Chicago public schools, governs the school, evaluates the principal, oversees the curriculum, and prepares the school budget. To improve their ability to serve on the LSC, members receive special training on effective meeting procedures.

Parents can become further involved at an annual three-day retreat where they can plan and design parent involvement activities with the school's educators. Parents are invited to this retreat only when they have attended at least eight school meetings and volunteered a minimum of three times a year.

CHAPTER 7

STANDARD VI: COLLABORATING WITH THE COMMUNITY

Definition: Community resources are used to strengthen schools, families, and student learning.

AS THE TITLE OF THIS BOOK SUGGESTS, it is important to establish effective partnerships that involve everyone in improving education and student success. Up to this point, the book has, for the most part, focused on how the National Standards for Parent/Family Involvement Programs can build a sense of community by forming partnerships among parents, school staff, and educators. The sixth and final standard, however, broadens this focus to engaging the greater community in effective partnerships with the school.

DEFINING "COMMUNITY" AND "PARTNERSHIPS"

Many people live in areas that are communities in name only. These so-called communities become *actual* communities only when their members—families, schools, corporations, colleges and universities, community agencies, and businesses—begin to discuss the importance of establishing a common identity and responsibility to each

other. Too often these different groups of people inhabit the same geo-
graphic area, but rarely spend time together and feel no real ties to each
other. For a real community to exist, its members must share a unified
purpose.

Partnerships can be relationships between several or more people or
groups. Like communities, partnerships such as coalitions, collabora-
tions, or connections among school, family, and community can only
truly exist when community members take the following steps (Kibel &
Stein-Seroussi, 1997):

1. Identify themselves by joint efforts with others striving for the
   same goal

2. Acknowledge their importance to and concern for each other

3. Profess common beliefs and shared values

4. Come together to bond and network

5. Accept mutual responsibility for sustaining and enhancing the
   quality of interrelationships between members

These five steps unleash the power of partnerships. The best partnerships are mutually beneficial and structured to connect individuals,
not just institutions or groups. When schools and communities work
together, both are synergistically strengthened and make gains that
outpace what either could accomplish on its own. Community efforts
to strengthen parent involvement pay off in many ways. For example,
parents involved with their children's education better understand the
need for paying taxes to fund schools. Residents involved with schools
tend to stay in a community longer, thus attracting higher-paying businesses, which increases local tax revenues (U.S. Department of Education, 1994).

The familiar African proverb, "It takes a village to raise a child," still
holds true today. Acclaimed child psychiatrist and urban school reform
proponent James P. Comer put it into more modern terms when he said
in his keynote address at the 1998 National PTA convention in

Nashville, Tennessee, that student success can be realized only with "the full participation of the community."

In the past, the "little red schoolhouse" served many purposes, and communities viewed it as their own. Today's modern urbanization has contributed to people feeling disconnected from each other and from their local schools. Recently, however, the idea of schools as community centers is being revitalized across the country. In New York City, the Beacons Schools serve as community learning centers. They offer sports and recreation, vocational training, and other services for students, community members, and parents during the school day, the evenings, and on weekends. In 1999, $450 million of federal funds was allocated to 21st Century Community Learning Centers, a federal program that funds school-based before- and after-school programs. (For more information on 21st Century Community Learning Centers, see chapter 9, page 179.) Across the nation, schools are converting to year-round schedules that include evening and weekend hours for school/community activities. Through these programs, the schoolhouse is regaining its place in the community and in people's hearts. According to a year-long study in 1998 by the Council of 21, commissioned by the American Association of School Administrators (1999), schools in the future will become nerve centers that connect teachers, students, and the community to the world's wealth of knowledge.

RESEARCH FINDINGS

Research on this subject shows that effective school, family, and community partnerships can provide the following benefits (Epstein et al., 1997; National PTA, 1998a):

Students

- Gain skills and talents from enriched curricular and extracurricular activities

- Develop positive relationships with adults other than their parents and teachers

- Feel a sense of value and belonging to the community

Parents

- Gain an awareness of the community's contributions to the school

- Develop a sense of connection with other families in the community

- Gain knowledge of and use local resources to obtain needed services, improve their skills, or both

Teachers and Administrators

- Gain knowledge of and become involved in the social and community service referral process for families with specific needs

- Develop skills for working with business partners, community volunteers, and mentors

- Gain knowledge of and use community resources to enrich classroom instruction

Community Agencies, Organizations, and Businesses

- Gain improved access to community resources

- Form connections between businesses and prospective future employees

- Gain a greater sense of purpose by contributing their wisdom to students

DIFFERENCES IN THE RESEARCH

While all the above research findings are true, it is important to be aware that various studies define parent involvement differently. This can make it hard for researchers to interpret the studies' results, according to Nancy Feyl Chavkin, a professor of social work and the co-director of the Center for Children and Families at the School of Health Professions at Southwest Texas State University.

Chavkin (1998) states that research studies differ in defining various aspects of parent involvement, such as where it takes place, in what ways, and how often. Some studies also vary in how they assess the outcome of parent involvement. For example, some studies look at improved academic achievement, while others look at improved school climate. Thus, while researchers are using the same words, they may actually be saying different things.

Joyce Epstein, the director of the Center on School, Family, and Community Partnerships at Johns Hopkins University, agrees with Chavkin. However, Epstein believes that despite problems with current data and research in this area, we still can be reasonably sure that school, family, and community partnerships can help students succeed. She bases her certainty on results from studies that have looked at the *process* of partnership activities in schools. When researchers have studied the process, they have found that despite the different definitions and variables used in some studies, community partnerships benefit students (Epstein, 1995).

One such study was conducted by Thomas Hatch (1998), a senior scholar at Harvard Project Zero, Carnegie Foundation for the Advancement of Teaching. Hatch studied the community involvement practices of three schools and the resulting improvements in test scores among students. Although he admits that it is difficult to pinpoint exactly how partnerships contribute to improved test scores, he suggests that schools with strong community partnerships show some common patterns that have led to increased test scores through a type of beneficial chain reaction.

According to Hatch, one of the things that can trigger this type of chain reaction is parents and community members taking action to make basic school improvements. For example, when parents, teachers, and community members improve a school's physical condition and resources, such as repainting the school or fixing broken equipment, they begin to feel a sense of ownership. This begins to change the attitudes and expectations of teachers and students as well as other parents and community members. The growing sense of collaboration, ownership, and pride can then motivate the principal to encourage teachers to try new instructional approaches and pursue training and resources to improve the curriculum. Overall, the quality and depth of the learning experience improves, and students' test scores go up.

BARRIERS TO FORMING PARTNERSHIPS

Two of the most common barriers to forming community partnerships are social differences and the lack of time.

Bridging Social Distances

Communities are often split along racial, class, and ethnic lines. To define common goals and create an effective community partnership, however, all stakeholders must be respected and included. Educators, parents, and business leaders need to reach beyond their comfort zones; step outside of their homes, classrooms, or offices; and work with people from different socioeconomic backgrounds. Biases and prejudices should be honestly discussed and worked through at the beginning of the partnership so that meaningful collaboration can occur.

Finding Time

There never seems to be enough time to do all the things we want and need to do. Most teachers already feel stretched beyond their limits. Parents, too, feel overwhelmed by the demands of their jobs, families, homes, schools, and communities. Schools, families, and community members need to work together to find ways of using both time and community resources more effectively to support each other. Time constraints can be addressed and overcome through the process described below.

STEPS TO FORMING COMMUNITY PARTNERSHIPS

Research indicates that community partnerships are one of the best ways to effect local change. To begin a partnership, an alliance must be formed among various community groups. This is not always easy to do. For example, in many communities, school administrators remain separate from PTAs. This is unfortunate, because administrators have valuable contributions to make, as do parents and teachers. When school administrators and PTA members work together, the PTA can become a strong and multi-voiced organization that can play a leadership role in forming coalitions to address specific issues. As partners, administrators and PTA members can support and reinforce each other's goals, thus strengthening one another while serving the larger community.

The following steps provide an outline for creating home-school-community partnerships that can be applied to any community's efforts:

1. Conduct a community needs assessment study to find out how best to serve the community.

2. PTA members, school administrators, and educators should develop a list of social service organization members and business and community leaders to approach about joining them on an *action team*. You can consider those individuals you have successfully worked with in the past and those who support the PTA's or school's mission. These prospective team members should also be respected in the community, and be concerned about and have a stake in the issues to be addressed by the committee.

3. Once you have selected team members, get together with them informally to plan an official *community meeting*. Determine the format and logistics—the when, where, and how——of this first official community meeting. Be sure to include the following steps:

    •   Establish an agenda. The agenda should identify the community's priority issues and needs to be addressed at the meeting. The team then should decide upon some realistic goals that it hopes to achieve at the community meeting.

    •   Collect the financial and material resources needed for a successful meeting.

    •   Select guest speakers for the first meeting who can address the major issues of concern.

    •   Decide how future action team meetings should be conducted by establishing ground rules, communication procedures, etc.

- Before sending out invitations to the community meeting, take steps to create a promotional plan to develop interest and support in the community for the action team and its mission. You should also develop a media plan to advertise the community meeting.

4. At the action team's first official community meeting, focus on the specific issues previously identified, and set mutual goals for the partnership. Discussion then should focus on developing an action plan to support and meet the team's goals and carry out its plans. Developing action teams and plans is discussed in detail in chapter 9.

5. Following the first official meeting, the team should send thank-you notes to speakers. All those who attended the meeting should receive follow-up material summarizing what was discussed and the commitments that were made. Once an action plan is in motion, additional meetings and follow-up activities can be scheduled to report on progress, evaluate the project, make further plans, and eventually begin future projects.

QUALITY TIPS FOR SUCCESSFUL PROGRAMS

Any coalition among parents, educators, community organization members, social agency members, and business members can use the following strategies for establishing effective partnerships that serve the whole community:

- Distribute information regarding cultural, recreational, academic, health, social, and other resources that serve families within the community.

- Inform school staff of the resources available in the community and of the best way to use them.

- Use community resources, materials, and people to enhance and enrich the school's curriculum.

- Foster student participation in community service.

- Involve community members in school volunteer programs.

- Disseminate information about school programs and perform-ance to the residents of the school's community, including those without school-age children.

BUILDING PARTNERSHIPS WITH COMMUNITY GROUPS

In every community, there is an almost endless array of groups with which schools can form partnerships. Social service agencies, religious organizations, school boards, businesses, neighborhood associations, and city or county agencies are but a few. It is beyond the scope of this book to discuss all of the possible community groups you could partner with. This chapter focuses on the two groups that may offer the best potential in most communities to give resources and support—busi-nesses and universities.

Building Partnerships With Businesses

According to recent statistics from the U.S. Bureau of Labor, 70% of employed parents spend more than 40 hours a week on their jobs. These employees feel that they do not have enough time to be involved with their children and families (Galinsky et al., 1995, p. 4). A number of ini-tiatives have tried to influence employers to be more family friendly. Among them are the U.S. Department of Education's Partnership for Family Involvement in Education—which is a national coalition of fam-ilies/schools, businesses, and religious communities—and President Clinton's speech, "Call to Action for American Education in the 21st Century," in which he challenges community stakeholders to improve schools by strengthening family involvement in learning.

Today's students are tomorrow's employees. This means that busi-nesses have a direct and immediate stake in improving education and student achievement. PTA members and principals working together can involve business members on partnership teams and can help them understand the value of parent involvement at school and its effect on student achievement. Educators can urge employers to form partner-ships with parents and adopt family-friendly policies that benefit schools and students. In the long run, these policies will also benefit companies, because competent, happy employees are more productive.

Some of the family-friendly policies employers can implement are flex time, part-time work options, and telecommuting. Employers can also offer time off for school meetings and special activities, as well as on-site child care, lunch-time seminars on parenting, and parent training programs. These types of programs allow parents to be more involved in their children's learning (Galinsky et al., 1995; Gary, Barbara, Marburger, & Witherspoon, 1996; The Conference Board, 1997). PTAs and the school community can also form partnerships with businesses to provide resources—such as computers, textbooks, field trips, and tutoring programs—that enhance the school's curriculum. Other examples of school/business partnership activities include career days, mentoring programs, internships, and school-to-work programs.

School-business relationships based on sound principles can have positive effects and contribute to high-quality education. Together, parents and educators can use the following principles to establish guidelines for corporate involvement in schools. These guidelines are from the National PTA's corporate sponsorship policy and resolution, "Commercial Exploitation of Students in Schools."

- Corporate involvement must support the goals and objectives of the schools. Curriculum and instruction are within the purview of educators.

- Corporate involvement programs must be structured to meet an identified need; linked to specific activities, events, and programs—not a commercial motive; and evaluated for effectiveness by the school or district on an ongoing basis.

- Because school property and time are publicly funded, corporate involvement should not sell or provide free access to advertisements on school property or require students to observe, listen, or read commercial advertising as a condition of the school receiving a donation of money or equipment.

- Educators should hold sponsored and donated materials to the same standards used for the selection and purchase of other school-related materials. The materials should offer balanced and diverse views.

- Corporate involvement programs should not limit the discretion of educators in the use of sponsored materials.

- Sponsor recognition and corporate logos should be used for identification rather than commercial purposes.

Building Partnerships With Colleges and Universities

Student-community relationships and partnerships with colleges are growing. A partnership between the community and the university can enhance college students' development both personally and professionally. These partnerships create direct links between the theoretical work in the classroom and real-life issues that organizations such as schools address daily. These links are the essence of *service learning*. In cooperation with local schools, college students can apply their knowledge and skills to solving some of the problems schools face, such as violence, truancy, and dropouts (Palm & Toma, 1997).

Community service learning projects allow university, elementary, and secondary students to benefit from interaction with each other. Groups of students can expand their worldviews and gain new skills and interests that can help them make more informed future career decisions. In the long run, service learning projects can also benefit society at large. According to Palm and Toma, "Students who have had service learning experiences are more likely to engage in social issues and give back to the community" (1997, p. 64). Some schools are making participation in community projects a graduation requirement. Through these long-term partnerships, university students can function as tutors, academic and career mentors, classroom speakers, and student teachers. Some universities also collaborate with the community service programs of the local middle and high schools and work together with students on projects in areas such as conservation and community outreach.

College and university alumni can also act as informal advisors, mentors, or community advisory council members. Alumni working in local businesses can be instrumental in arranging internships and work-study programs for current students.

Successful long-term partnerships involve coordination, support, and supervision of community projects by both local schools and universities. Lasting relationships should be based on formal, mutually developed, and ongoing contracts that define the duties and responsibilities of everyone involved.

PROJECT IDEAS

Ideas for PTAs and the School Community Working Together

ONE GOOD DEED DESERVES ANOTHER. Take the first step in creating partnerships with other community groups—such as the YMCA, the Boy and Girl Scouts, and the chamber of commerce—by sending PTA ambassadors to help out in one of their annual events or programs. By working together, these groups can become familiar with what each has to offer to the community. This can lead to these groups collaborating to create brochures for parents about resources and activities for children during non-school hours.

"HEALTHY" PARTNERSHIPS. Invite local hospital and health department officials to sponsor a health fair or a free clinic-on-wheels. Fairs and clinics can provide health and nutrition information, information on children's health issues and available services, immunizations for children, and demonstrations of emergency care and safety techniques by hospital personnel or paramedics.

GIVE-BACK DAYS. Sponsor annual "Give-Back" days to encourage students to go out into the community and perform needed work or services. Coordinate student activities with local authorities, such as chambers of commerce or city councils, to find the most appropriate and beneficial services that would allow students to give back to the community.

GET THE WORD OUT. Work with community agencies to distribute a twice-yearly community newsletter with pertinent information about their services, local businesses, and special community events. Create brochures for real estate agents to distribute to prospective residents that highlight what local schools have to offer, or use the local cable access station to promote parent involvement in school. You can also use the local newspaper for publicity. Ask a reporter to write about your school's PTA, or ask the school district superintendent to write a letter to the editor calling for employer cooperation and encouraging parents to attend parent-teacher conferences and other parent involvement activities. Include a page on your school's website or community website to promote the benefits of parent involvement.

Ideas for Coordinating Community Services

"CALL US. WE'RE IN THE BOOK." Develop a directory of social and community service agencies that includes program descriptions, addresses, phone numbers, e-mail addresses, website addresses, and names of contact people. Distribute the directory, and make it available online to parents, teachers, counselors, and the principal.

WHERE TO GO FOR WHAT. In conjunction with social and community service representatives, establish a service referral committee or a family center in the school or community. The committee or center should provide information on where to go for training, support, and child-care resources; food, clothing, and shelter; and referrals for mental health, medical, and other community services. The center could also provide free pamphlets, brochures, and tip sheets on parenting.

FAMILY MEETINGS. Schedule informational meetings for families at school or in the community. Invite social service representatives to meet with families and talk about topics such as Social Security, Aid to Families with Dependent Children, food stamps, available health services, and so forth.

Ideas for Working With Businesses

PARTNERING WITH PTA. Businesses can develop partnerships with PTAs by sponsoring PTA events, hosting PTA meetings, and holding on-site parent-teacher conferences.

AN ENVELOPE THEY'RE SURE TO OPEN. With educators from local schools, develop paycheck-size cards with tips on how parents can help their children succeed. Include the cards with employees' paychecks.

HOSTING THE COMMUNITY. Bring the school and the community into the workplace with student performances or community service fairs that are held at different times during the day. You can also sponsor community resources workshops for teachers during the summer to help them learn about the educational, cultural, and business resources in the community.

Ideas for Teachers

STUDENT PROJECT PAIRS. Ask older students to help mentor younger students by doing projects together. Set aside special days for classrooms to participate in joint activities.

CHARITY ON THE RUNWAY. Work with a local charity to host a fashion or talent show and to integrate the activities into students' course work. Invite parents and community members to the show, and donate the proceeds to the cooperating charity.

SCHOOL-TO-WORK SUPPORT. As part of a work-study or school-to-work program, take parents on tours of internship or apprenticeship sites.

Ideas for PTAs Working With Middle and High School Communities

LEARNING BY HELPING. Create service learning programs that allow students flexibility in choosing assignments and initiating contacts that are directly tied to their regular curriculum. For example, these programs could be in nursing homes, food pantries, or homes for disabled children. Teachers should be involved in designing and supervising these experiences. Ask students to keep journals of their experiences, to share what they are doing and learning on a weekly basis, and to write a summary report at the end of the project.

GIVING STUDENTS A VOICE. Elect several student representatives to community advisory boards or councils. Send information to parents and students describing the commitment this activity would require and the skills students would gain from the experience. Teachers, principals, and community members can choose student representatives by judging essays or presentations from interested students on why they should be chosen for the committee. Once elected, students should receive training and orientation from the community advisory council, which could include mentoring as well as teaching them about the history, mission, goals, and responsibilities of the council. Students should also be provided with information on upcoming council events and tasks, and be given ongoing support and transportation to the meetings if needed.

PARENTS R US. Form a partnership with a local day-care or Head Start program, and start a parent readiness program that gives high school students practical experiences in working with preschool children. Each student can be paired with a preschooler and the child's teacher for a semester to work together to strengthen particular areas of the child's development. This helps teens gain insight into their future roles as parents or teachers, as well as performing a community service.

GETTING BACK TO NATURE. Encourage student involvement in environmental community efforts such as studying and monitoring water quality and pollution, river or stream cleanup projects, recycling drives, tree planting, soil conservation, or wildlife restoration projects.

LIGHTS, CAMERA, ACTION! Produce a promotional video that provides information on school and community activities or a specific issue concerning the community. Local cable companies offer free video production classes as a part of their community service and to meet FCC regulations for programming. Alternatively, you might produce a pamphlet or write an article in the school or community newspaper.

BEST PRACTICES

Each community and each set of volunteers are unique. These programs should be considered as guidelines. If you think a program might work for you, adapt it to your situation.

Publix Works

The mission statement of Publix Super Markets, Inc., emphasizes its role as a responsible corporate citizen and establishes its philosophy for educational support through community involvement. This support for education has been the cornerstone of the community involvement efforts of Publix's 580 stores throughout Alabama, Florida, Georgia, and South Carolina.

One way the company supports education is through Publix Educational Partnerships (PEP). PEP was created in 1995 to unify and organize a multitude of educational support activities within the company. PEP's major components are store-work partnerships, career education and store tours, school-to-work initiatives, and corporate office school volunteer initiatives. Through its personnel policies, Publix also encourages employee involvement in local schools. The Florida education commissioner has credited Publix with increasing volunteerism in Florida by 20% (EdPress media kit, November 11, 1998).

In its school-to-work program, Publix explains its career opportunities and benefits to students as well as its job needs and expectations so that future applicants know what it takes to be a qualified applicant in that job market. Publix also has a job-shadowing program. For example, in Miami Gardens Elementary School in Florida, students were selected to shadow a Publix store manager as he made his rounds to monitor the store's various departments. During the job shadowing, students were able to talk to each of the department managers about their jobs' roles and responsibilities.

Publix was one of the first companies honored with a Star Award for Business Leadership when the award program began in 1998. Sponsored by EdPress, the Association for Educational Publishers, this award recognizes the efforts of a company to improve the quality of life through education, though its business lies mainly in other fields.

Helping in Rural Communities

Children in rural communities often do not have places to go after school where they can find constructive activities, a safe environment, and caring adult help. Three organizations—Save the Children, the National Institute for Out-of-School Time, and Aguirre International— have teamed up to form the Save the Children Out-of-School Time Rural Initiative, which has programs in several rural communities.

The initiative funds the Family Learning Center in El Rito, New Mexico, where children are offered after-school and summer programs with activities such as art and computer lab instruction. The center provides a safe and stimulating place for both younger and older children, and it serves as a meeting place for the social, cultural, and educational activities of many community groups.

The initiative also funds the Youth Development Program in Chinle, Arizona, which promotes self-esteem and addresses issues that the area's youth face, such as drugs, gangs, employment skills, and puberty. About 500 youth participate in the program's educational and recreational activities, which include sports, survival camp, and peer tutoring.

In Zuni, New Mexico, some of the Zuni School District's after-school and summer programs are also funded by the initiative. One of the programs is the Family Book Bag Project, in which families may check out bags of books, participate in community read-a-thons, and attend workshops that are held by guest authors and illustrators. Children may also participate in the Summer Arts and Reading Program, which promotes recreational reading.

PUTting Out Effort

In Fort Worth, Texas, an entire community is working to improve an area middle school through Operation PUT (Parents United with Teachers), a joint effort of ACT (Allied Communities of Tarrant) and school faculty. ACT is sponsored by the Texas Interfaith Education Fund (TIEF), a statewide program that brings together parents, residents, church members, business and community leaders, and educators to focus on improving the public school system. The program's goals are to involve parents in school, make the school the center of the community, improve student achievement, and reduce the dropout rate.

Formed in 1987, ACT has served as a catalyst for bringing together community members to help improve public education. The group chose to start one of the first parent involvement programs at Morningside Middle School of Fort Worth, Texas, because the school's principal was committed to parent involvement and the school had low test scores, low levels of achievement, and a very high dropout rate. Seventy-five percent of the school's students are from low-income families.

Through ACT, several church committees have become active in improving Morningside. These committees include a Pastor Education Committee, whose purpose is to keep organizers and project participants effectively communicating; a Church Education Committee, which includes two members of each neighborhood church and works to further communication between the churches and the project; and a Church Visitation Group, which is responsible for grassroots organizing efforts.

The only full-time staff working on Operation PUT is an education coordinator, who is assisted by numerous community volunteers. The education coordinator has helped design and start a plan to visit every Morningside family to inform them about the program and tell them how to become involved with their children's school. The visit also helps ACT members understand the families and how they feel about their school.

Big Help

For elementary-age children to help the community, they often must be shown the way. In April 1998, children in six Chicago elementary schools were given such help by the Chicago Region PTA and the Big Help program of the children's cable station Nickelodeon.

PTA members contacted Nickelodeon about Big Help, and Nickelodeon sent a kit that contained videos and other materials to help PTAs assist students in preparing and implementing community service projects. The Big Help week in April began with a visit from the Big Helpmobile, which visited all participating Chicago schools. Students toured the Big Helpmobile trailer, received goodie bags, had their photos taken, and talked with Nickelodeon staff members.

The Big Help program continued with each of the six participating schools tackling a different project. The projects included collecting toiletries, food, school supplies, and other items for local homeless shelters; cleaning up around the school or a local park; adopting a children's unit at a hospital by collecting toys and making cards for the patients; adopting the local Boys and Girls Club and helping out with volunteer work for the year; and adopting nursing home residents by making them cards and baskets.

TEAM Winner

In 1998, the PTA at Fort Gordon, Georgia, which is in an open military post, won the National PTA's local TEAM (Together Everyone Achieves Membership) Award for community awareness. The Fort Gordon PTA educated the military community as well as local, state, regional, and national audiences about PTA and child-related issues by using three strategies: information sharing, partnerships, and outreach programs.

The information-sharing strategy focused on educating people about PTA and military family issues and encouraging united community action. Using the local media, newsletters, and posters, the PTA members promoted their workshops to community members on a variety of topics such as Working Together for Stronger Communities, Developing Volunteer Leaders, Fort Gordon Community Partnerships, and Quality Business Partnerships.

For the partnership strategy, PTA members teamed up with the local library staff to promote a summer reading program. Together they worked to increase materials funding, participation, awareness, and programming for all children. The program provided children with a variety of craft activities, story time and storytelling events, and field trip story sessions.

The outreach strategy consisted of a program that encouraged safe and appropriate technology use and parent/community involvement in technology planning. PTA members collaborated with business and community members to conduct classes and presentations to help parents, children, and community residents learn about online resources and other technologies.

CHAPTER 8

OVERCOMING BARRIERS AND REACHING OUT TO KEY PLAYERS

MOST PARENTS WANT TO BE INVOLVED in their children's education, and most administrators and educators recognize the importance of parent involvement to a student's success. Even so, the many barriers to developing successful parent involvement programs can make even simple programs difficult to create and maintain. These barriers can be overcome, however, when educators, PTA members, and parents work together.

Several recent surveys have found that educators and parents generally agree that children do better in school when parents are involved in their education. In December 1998, the National PTA, in conjunction with the public opinion research firm Bennett, Petts, and Blumenthal, conducted a telephone survey of 800 parents of public school children from across the county. The survey examined parents' views of public education and parent involvement in schools. Ninety-one percent of parents polled felt it was extremely important for parents to be involved in their children's education (National PTA, 1998b, pp. 5, 7).

This finding was also supported in a 1999 study by Public Agenda, a research organization that works to help average citizens better understand policy issues and the nation's leaders better understand the public's viewpoint. This study included a telephone survey of 1,220 parents whose children were in grades K–12 and a mail survey of 1,000 K–12 public school teachers on their views of parent involvement in public schools. Eighty-one percent of teachers surveyed felt that it is very hard for children to succeed in school without involved parents (Public Agenda, 1999, p. 43) Seventy-two percent of parents felt that "kids can sometimes get shortchanged and fall through the cracks" when their parents are not involved at school (p. 43). These studies support findings from earlier studies done by Newsweek Inc., Chrysler, and the National PTA (1990, 1991, 1993).

In the National PTA survey, 58% of parents polled strongly agreed that families were encouraged to volunteer for school activities as well as help their children with homework; 57% strongly felt that teachers at their children's school welcomed their involvement (National PTA, 1998b, p. 57). Parents who had a less positive assessment of educators' outreach efforts were those of high school-aged children, working mothers, and parents who were not involved with a parent-teacher organization.

Despite these positive findings, only 29% of the parents polled in the PTA survey felt that teachers and principals had a lot of good ideas about how to involve parents, and only 38% felt that they actually had a lot of input in their children's education (p. 57). In the Public Agenda survey, 98% of teachers (Public Agenda, 1999, p. 43) and 87% of parents felt that "it is always the same group of parents who are involved in school activities" (p. 38).

As these studies suggest, it is not a lack of interest that keeps parents and families from becoming involved in their children's education. Often, there are genuine barriers blocking the way to positive parent involvement. The challenge is to overcome these barriers and help parents become meaningful contributors and supporters.

BARRIERS TO PARENT INVOLVEMENT: ROADBLOCKS AND DETOURS

Administrators, educators, parents, and PTA members need to work together to find detours around the roadblocks that present barriers to effective parent involvement programs. A few of the more common roadblocks, and suggested detours around them, are presented below.

Not Having Enough Time

ROADBLOCK: Parents often cite time as the single greatest barrier to volunteering, attending meetings, and joining decision-making committees at their children's school. These activities often are scheduled at times that interfere with work or other obligations.

DETOUR: Be flexible and creative in scheduling meetings and events. Try a mix of mornings, evenings, and weekends to allow every parent the opportunity to attend. Consider potluck dinners and brown-bag lunches to meet the needs of working parents. Hold meetings at community centers, apartment buildings, church halls, parks, libraries, and the workplace to make it easier for parents to attend. Sponsor monthly community family events and use part of the time to give information to parents and discuss important issues.

Not Feeling Valued

ROADBLOCK: Some parents are not sure they have anything of value to contribute. They may also feel intimidated by principals, teachers, and PTA leaders. These parents may have had unpleasant school experiences or may have limited education or low literacy levels. Parents whose experience with the law has been negative may also be reluctant or embarrassed to participate in some schools or programs that now require the fingerprinting of regular volunteers. Educators and administrators can reinforce these feelings if they give the impression that they think uninvolved parents lack in certain qualities or are deficient in some way.

DETOUR: Extend a personal welcome to parents who appear to be withdrawn or uncomfortable. Establish regular communication to build relationships based on mutual respect and trust. This kind of relation-ship can help shed light on family issues (e.g., family illness, aging par-ent, financial stress) that may affect a parent's ability to participate in school activities. Learn about parents' interests and abilities, actively seek opportunities at home or at school for them to use their experience and talents to benefit the school in some way, and then value each and every contribution. For parents with low literacy levels, schools can make phone calls, home visits, or provide video messages. Schools can also work with local libraries to form literacy groups and provide adult literacy and programs teaching English as a second language.

Feeling Unwelcome

ROADBLOCK: Parents may feel they are unwelcome in the school. Staff interactions, attitudes, and the physical appearance of some schools may convey an unwelcoming environment.

DETOUR: Provide in-service training for all faculty and staff to help them become aware of the importance of parent involvement and acquire the knowledge and skills needed to successfully interact with parents. Tell parents that they are welcome to visit during the school day and that measures such as visitor passes are there for security reasons—not to make them feel unwelcome. To make parent visitors feel more comfortable, post welcome signs in all languages spoken at the school at each entrance and on each classroom door. Create a special place in the school that is set aside especially for parents, such as a parent center.

Not Knowing How to Contribute

ROADBLOCK: Some parents believe they have talents, but do not know whether those talents are needed or how to contribute them to the school or the PTA.

DETOUR: Do not wait for parents to offer to help; seek them out. Have teachers and administrators meet to create a list of qualities and contributions needed from parents. Hold a parent meeting or conduct a survey to determine the kinds of teacher support and school policies parents think are necessary for positive parent involvement. Faculty and parents can then share their lists with each other and begin to discuss how to more effectively use parents' many talents.

Not Understanding the School System

ROADBLOCK: Many parents are unfamiliar with the school system and do not know what rights they have or how they can become involved.

DETOUR: Create a parent handbook that explains rules, procedures, policies, and where to find answers to questions. Include the names and numbers of contact people who can answer questions in specific areas. Include the pictures and names of school administrators, staff, teachers, PTA officers, and other contact people.

Parents in Need

ROADBLOCK: Parents without adequate resources often feel overwhelmed. Families suffering from economic stress must first meet their own needs for food, clothing, and shelter before they can become more involved in their children's education.

DETOUR: Provide information to help parents secure the health and social services they need for themselves and their families. Schools can work out agreements with social and health agencies to provide services through school-based clinics or community-based clinics that are near the school. Schools can also develop and distribute to parents a directory containing information on available services and resources in the community and how to access them. After families' personal needs are met, schools can then help parents become involved in the their children's education.

Lack of Child Care

ROADBLOCK: Child care may not routinely be offered at meetings or school functions. At the same time, parents may be discouraged from bringing their children to such events.

DETOUR: Find an available room for child care at the meeting site. Ask PTA members, community members, school service clubs, or other parents to volunteer to provide child care on a rotating basis. Another option is to provide child care by hiring high school or college students in child development classes or child-care professionals in the community and, if appropriate, charging parents a nominal fee. Adhere to state-mandated child/adult ratios to provide safe, quality care.

Language Barriers

ROADBLOCK: Parents who do not speak English may not understand newsletters, fliers, or speakers at meetings.

DETOUR: Make sure that all printed materials that are sent home and distributed at meetings are published in all of the languages spoken by the families in the school. The school and surrounding community may also need to identify and help secure interpreters and translators for workshops and meetings. Another option is to begin group activities and social times in the same room and then have parents of the same language group break off into smaller groups in different rooms for more in-depth discussion. Have all parents come together at the end of the meeting and have the bilingual reporter for each group share what was discussed.

Special Needs

ROADBLOCK: Parents with disabilities may feel uncomfortable or be unable to attend and contribute at meetings.

DETOUR: Make sure your school is accessible for everyone, and hold meetings or events in a space that can accommodate parents with disabilities. Provide someone to sign for deaf or hearing-impaired parents.

Lack of Transportation

ROADBLOCK: Lack of transportation or access to parking at the school may keep parents from visiting or attending school activities.

DETOUR: Work with the school to make available a block of spaces in the parking lot "for visitors only." Have school buses transport parents to special evening events, following regular bus routes or stopping at designated places for group pickups and drop-offs. Form carpools to provide transportation for parents without cars. Hold events in community locations that are easy to access and are near public transportation. If parents cannot attend, provide a home visit or a phone call to keep them updated and involved.

BARRIERS FOR PTAS TO OVERCOME

If PTAs are to uphold the PTA Mission (see page 235), it is important that they try to overcome barriers that keep parents from being involved in meaningful ways. Below are examples of specific barriers and ways that one PTA is trying to overcome them. These examples have been taken from ma-terial developed by the San Diego Unified PTA Council's Project Hope.

Snobbery and Exclusion

ROADBLOCKS: Many parents still view PTA or other parent groups as isolated and established cliques that exclude minorities and newcomers. This image can be a turnoff to both new parents and diverse groups within the school community.

DETOUR: Actively seek new members that represent the entire school community. Barriers to outreach—such as insensitivity to a particular group—cannot be adequately addressed and discussed without representatives of that group on school committees or in parent groups. Talk with other organizations, read books, or attend workshops to find appropriate ways to reach out to specific populations and make your school groups more inclusive.

Resistance to Change

ROADBLOCK: Some PTA members, school administrators, and teachers may resist the idea of PTAs assuming roles other than providing hospitality and financial support for school needs.

DETOUR: The National PTA was founded more than 100 years ago with a mission to advocate for and educate others on issues affecting children and families. PTA leaders at all levels should look at current PTA rules and customs that may hinder effective parent involvement and interfere with the PTA's original purpose—to serve as an agent of change for children and families. PTAs need to work with educators to discuss how today's PTAs can involve parents in advocacy efforts and can create home-school partnerships that unite efforts to meet the needs of parents and children.

Lack of Sufficient Training

ROADBLOCK: Many PTA leaders assume their positions with little or no advocacy or leadership experience.

DETOUR: Seek and provide ongoing training for PTA members at all levels in the areas of leadership, advocacy, communication, and the PTA philosophy so that they can effectively serve in their roles and accomplish the PTA mission.

REACHING OUT TO SPECIFIC POPULATIONS

If a school's goal is to increase parent involvement, then all parents need to be the target of the school's outreach efforts. Given the many kinds of families and caregivers that exist in the lives of children, schools need to be more sensitive to and creative in making all families feel included.

Culturally Diverse Families

Schools need to review the research and learn about families' cultural and social values and expectations regarding school systems. For example, some cultures entrust their children to the school and feel that it is inappropriate and insulting to teachers and principals for parents to interact with them (Klumpp, 1990). Developing a better understanding of families' cultures can help correct misconceptions and stereotypes and can make schools more sensitive to families' needs.

Schools can show respect for cultures by making an effort not to plan school events on religious and cultural holidays. Schools can also explain to parents how U.S. schools work, offer adults classes in English as a second language, help parents prepare for citizenship, and hold school events that share cultures through food and music. Ethnic community leaders should be included in school improvement efforts, and bilingual parents should be recruited, trained, and hired as paraprofessionals and liaisons to families (U.S. Department of Education, 1996). Any outreach provided to diverse families should focus on the family as a whole, promote a family's self-sufficiency, and emphasize their assets (Chang, Salazar, & Leong, 1994).

Fathers

Fathers are often overlooked in parent involvement programs, yet it is critical for schools to involve dads in meaningful ways in their children's education (Brimhall, West, & Winquist-Nord, 1997). In 2 million homes nationwide, fathers are the only parent living with their children (Byrson & Casper, 1998, p. 5). Schools need to try to include fathers in school events, meetings, conferences, and so forth, and actively seek a balance of mothers and fathers on all school committees. Furthermore, PTA members and educators can ask fathers to help form dads clubs and to recruit other men in the community as volunteers. To help fathers, PTAs and schools can encourage local employers to adopt family-friendly policies that would allow fathers the time to be more involved at their children's school.

Single and Working Parents

There are almost 15 million single-parent households nationwide (Bryson & Casper, 1998, p. 5). Due to divorce, death, and other reasons, an increasing number of children now live in single-parent and working-parent households. Schools should reach out to single parents in a variety of ways. For example, if a parent is not living in the same home as his or her children, educators can send information about the children and the school to both parents, and have joint or separate parent-teacher conferences with both parents. Schools can offer support groups and workshops to single parents to help them and their children cope with the stress of a separation, a divorce, or a death. PTA members can extend friendship and help to single parents by including them in carpools and child-care cooperatives and by offering them information about community services.

Schools can reach out to single and working parents by offering meetings, events, and conferences in the evenings or on weekends. Offering before- and after-school programs, potlucks, and brown bag lunches could also be helpful. PTAs and schools can also collaborate with area businesses and community leaders to obtain support from employers for employees to be involved in their schools. This could include involving these employees as aides to learning and mentors in reading and math one or two days a month.

REACHING OUT TO OTHER KEY PLAYERS

The investment, support, and commitment of all community stakeholders is essential for creating a strong and successful parent involvement program. How or if parents, educators, and school staff initially become involved can depend on what motivates them. Ideally, people are motivated to become involved either by a desire to help others succeed or by a need to understand and help others understand. Some people may also be motivated to become involved for the sense of accomplishment involvement provides. Still others will become involved only if there is a tangible incentive for them, such as higher pay or greater prestige. Unfortunately, some will not become involved at all, no matter what incentive is offered. These people may not want change, whether out of fear or other reasons of their own.

Motivating people to become involved and move partnerships forward takes a commitment to reach out, listen to each other, and work together. The support of school administrators, teachers, school board members, the superintendent, and other appointed or elected public officials in establishing a strong and effective parent involvement program is essential for its success. Members of each of these groups should be considered as partners who can make important and unique contributions to this process. Understanding these partners can help PTA members reach out to them.

Principals

The principal's leadership sets the tone and shapes the culture for the entire school. He or she has a pivotal role in establishing a foundation for individual school changes and successes. The principal's ideas and actions can provide the financial support and motivation needed to bring the entire school staff and faculty into the process of promoting strong parent-school-community partnerships.

PTA leaders can request to regularly meet with principals to keep them informed, seek their input on upcoming activities, discuss concerns and issues, and resolve problems and misunderstandings. PTAs can also work with principals by asking them to serve on their committees and by having PTA representatives serve on site-based management councils. In this way, PTAs can provide their input on annual reports and school budgets as well as be involved with writing policies and school codes, setting schoolwide goals, and planning programs to achieve those goals.

Two-way, ongoing communication is an important key to working with administrators. PTAs should consider the following three questions as they begin to establish partnerships with principals:

1. What can PTAs do to benefit all children and families at the school?

2. What can principals do to help PTAs accomplish their goals?

3. What can PTAs and principals do together to achieve success for all children and families?

A cooperative climate can be established by demonstrating a commitment to work with principals in areas that have traditionally been their sole responsibility. Showing this kind of support for an administrator can open the door to his or her reciprocal support of programs important to PTAs.

Teachers

Teachers are another crucial link in the partnership between schools and parents. Positive parent-teacher relationships enhance parent involvement and benefit teachers. Parents and teachers have much in common in their roles, but their approaches are often different. This difference sometimes leaves teachers feeling isolated from parents, and vice versa. Strong parent-teacher bonds, however, can help alleviate these feelings of isolation.

A PTA can provide a bridge between parents and teachers and can help build a positive relationship between the two groups. Some teachers, however, will not be as willing to participate in PTA as other teachers.

PTA members may want to work with the most responsive teachers first, because these teachers may be able to eventually draw in others with their success and accomplishments.

PTAs and principals need to acknowledge teachers' expertise and the enormity of their work, set reasonable goals for teacher participation, and then develop the relationship from there. PTAs and principals can advocate for teachers by helping the community understand the importance of supporting continuing professional education for teachers—especially training for teachers in parent involvement and in shared decision making. When teachers feel supported in these fundamental ways, they become more receptive to actively working with groups such as a PTA. Then PTAs and teachers can work together to support the development of parent-teacher relationships. PTAs can provide informal occasions for teachers and parents to get to know each other as individuals and partners. PTAs can further strengthen parent-teacher communication and understanding by providing newsletters, workshops, events, and activities that bring these two groups together on a regular basis.

The School Board

Through long-range planning and goal setting, the school board is responsible for the activities and services of the schools and for the educational programs of the district. School boards are legally responsible for the policies and procedures that govern the operation of the entire school district. School boards are responsible for taking the lead in identifying and meeting the community's education needs through the adoption of local school policy. The school board is the policy-making body of the school system. Because the support of the school board is crucial to moving a parent/family involvement agenda forward and adopting a districtwide parent/family involvement policy, PTAs need to effectively reach out to this group.

PTAs can reach out to a school board by asking its members to help plan or attend PTA conferences, workshops, and programs. This will help board members gain a better understanding of the purpose and importance of PTA's work. PTAs can invite school board members to participate in PTA meetings and committees. PTA members can also appoint a liaison to attend school board meetings and ask to serve on school board advisory committees in order to communicate their concerns, become active in the decision-making process, and bring back information on current issues that may require PTA study and action. When liaisons introduce themselves and explain their role at the first board meeting, they begin to lay the groundwork for improving the relationship between the two groups. Liaisons can also encourage parents to attend meetings and become knowledgeable and involved in the school board election process. School boards can do a better job of meeting community needs when they are supported and challenged by a well-informed and involved community.

The Superintendent

Even if a PTA establishes a good relationship with the school board and is welcomed at board meetings and planning sessions, the success of all these efforts can be affected by the openness and influence of the superintendent. As chief executive officer of the school district, the superintendent is the education leader of the entire community. He or she interacts with the school board, principals, teachers, and parents, and ultimately sets the tone for how the school district as a whole responds to parents and families. Although the school board makes the policies, the superintendent supports the development of districtwide policies and helps the board identify goals for the schools. The superintendent also interprets how policies will be used to support principals and teachers, and he or she creates a school culture that will affect how parents are viewed and treated. Having the support of the superintendent promotes good site-based decision making with active parent involvement. The PTA is a critical element in this process because it joins together the voices of parents, teachers, and community members to influence the quality of education.

To effectively reach out and work with the superintendent, PTAs must understand and learn how to use administrative channels. For example, forming partnerships with the principal can lead to good working relationships with teachers, the school board, and others who shape our children's education. By developing a track record of strong working partnerships with these groups, the PTA can become more familiar with school policies and procedures and can develop a good understanding of the different roles and responsibilities of the principal, school board, and superintendent. These activities help the PTA gain credibility with and respect from the superintendent and give it a better chance of being heard as a key community leader.

Public Officials

PTAs' efforts to increase parent/family involvement in education can include reaching beyond their local school communities to include elected public officials. Because they are elected, public officials are generally concerned with listening and responding to their constituencies. Public officials speak for many and often have valuable connections. Elected or appointed officials may include mayors, city council members, state school superintendents and other state education department representatives, elected state representatives, and governors. These public officials have an important role in developing state and national policies and laws—that may create or remove barriers to parent/family involvement. Having the support of public officials can lead to the establishment of standards for parent involvement in education for local school communities to adopt and implement.

To effectively reach out to public officials, PTAs need to increase their sense of ownership in parent involvement issues. PTAs can do this by consulting with and seeking input from the policymakers who should be involved in local parent/family involvement efforts. PTAs should invite public officials to serve on their planning committees or respond to parent involvement plans. Public officials should be kept informed of what the PTA is doing locally, so that they understand the importance of PTA efforts and the long-term impact such efforts can have for schools and communities. One way to accomplish this is to host a back-to-school day for elected officials so they can have contact with local schools. Establishing this contact and communication can make it easier to discuss developing policies that support greater parent involvement. It can also make it easier to ask legislators at the local, state, and federal levels to sponsor these kinds of bills. Ultimately, PTAs want to establish a positive relationship with policymakers so that each group becomes a resource for the other.

EXPANDING THE ROLE AND IDEA OF LEADERSHIP

PTAs, principals, teachers, school boards, superintendents, and public officials all share a common goal—quality education. Any one person or group acting alone cannot achieve this goal. School leadership, then, must be considered within a broader context, which is separate from a particular person or role and embedded in the school community as a whole. This must be established through a shared sense of responsibility and purpose among all players at all levels (Lambert, 1998). Developing working partnerships with energy and purpose encourages others to learn collectively, collaborate and communicate with each other, and share decision making. The PTA and its partners can work toward establishing parent involvement at all levels of the education system to improve the education of all children.

We can think of the partnerships among all of these groups as a linked network, with the local PTAs at the center connecting with all the groups mentioned above. These partnerships operate within the larger network that represents the partnership the school has with the local community.

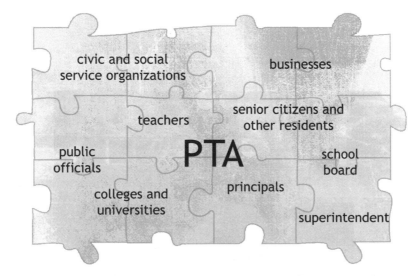

PTAs are often the link to connecting and building successful partnerships within a school and community network.

CHAPTER 9

ACTION TEAMS, PLANS, AND PARENT/FAMILY INVOLVEMENT POLICIES

THE BELIEF IN THE IMPORTANCE OF PARENTS and families is the starting point for all successful parent involvement programs. Knowing and understanding how to implement the National Standards, working to overcome barriers, and reaching out to key players in the system are also important parts of the process. This chapter will outline ways to turn interest and ideas into action through action teams, action plans, and parent/family involvement policies.

Parents who serve on action teams need to have regular and consistent access to other parents so that they can knowledgeably speak on their behalf and accurately represent the views of the parent community. However, parent involvement in this process should not be limited only to parents who serve on action teams. Creating an action team is just one of several steps in the process for initiating and maintaining the momentum needed for change. The following eight steps should be taken gradually to avoid a negative backlash from parents, the community, the school board, etc. Gradual, well-planned action can lead to real and lasting change.

1. Create an Action Team

Parents, educators, administrators, and others involved in education must be represented on an action team responsible for reaching a common understanding of the school's family involvement needs and setting mutual goals to meet them.

2. Examine Current Practice

Review the status of parent and family involvement in your school. Survey staff and parents to obtain a clear understanding of the current situation. The "Quality Tips for Successful Programs" sections in chapters 2–7 and the "Parent Involvement in Our Schools" survey in Appendix B are helpful tools for completing this process.

3. Develop an Improvement Plan

Based on an evaluation of current practices, identify priority issues and set goals. Include strategies for overcoming barriers, reaching out to key players, and developing a parent/family involvement policy. At this stage, you should identify and secure financial resources to fund the school's parent involvement initiatives.

4. Develop a Written Parent/Family Involvement Policy

A written parent/family involvement policy establishes the vision, mission, and foundation for future action plans. This chapter will discuss guidelines for developing such a policy and provide an example of a model policy statement.

5. Develop an Action Plan

Develop a plan for implementing the parent/family involvement policy within your school and district. Pay close attention to ensuring that the plan is comprehensive and well-balanced, and that it includes activities in each of the areas covered by the six National Standards.

6. Secure Support

For optimal success, make sure that those who will be responsible for implementing the plan, affected by the plan, or have influence over the plan's outcome are aware of the plan and willing to lend support to its success.

7. Provide Professional Development for School/Program Educators and Staff

Effective training on the parent/family involvement policy and action plan and on how to implement them for educators and staff, parents, and administrators is essential. The best models for training are those that provide educators and staff with several opportunities to become knowledgeable of and interact with the issues covered within the policy and plans. These models include opportunities for educators and staff to work together and become jointly responsible for monitoring and evaluating the progress of policy implementation.

8. Evaluate and Revise

Parent and family involvement is not a one time goal. It merits a process of continuous improvement and a commitment to long-term success. Plans and policies for involving parents and families should be evaluated and revised each school year.

DEVELOPING AN ACTION TEAM

To efficiently evaluate ideas and implement plans, a school community should form an action team (a parent involvement task force or committee). An action team is an energetic group of people committed to working together to achieve common goals and provide high-quality, planned results.

Action teams have two important roles:

1. To develop and draft a comprehensive, well-planned parent/ family involvement policy that addresses the six National Standards and

2. To develop action plans to implement the policy.

As discussed in the last chapter, school leadership responsibilities should be embraced by the school community as a whole. Initiatives can fail when this does not happen. For example, if a strong principal leaves

ACTION AND POLICIES

a school, parents and educators might lack the capacity to sustain the original efforts toward change. Teams should be made up of representatives of the entire school community: PTA members, administrators, school staff, community members, parents, and teachers representing all sectors of a school community, and, if appropriate, school board members and district administrators.

The term *capacity building* in current school reform strategies describes collaborative leadership. Leadership becomes a collective learning experience when all those involved with educating children share responsibility, thereby expanding the breadth of leadership to "skillful participation by many" (Lambert, 1998, p. 12). This environment of collaboration contributes to the development of a *leadership community* that can go forward even when individual members leave or move on. The chart on the following page illustrates the four stages of team development. The chart is adapted from Tuckman's Model of Group Development and was originally published in 1995 in National PTA's guide, *Parent Plus.*

Four Stages of Team Development

STAGE I. Stage I is a time of transition for group members. They need to identify the tasks of the team and address the issues of time and resources that contribute to meeting goals. Because team members may be hesitant to participate due to unfamiliar group dynamics and fear of rejection, a minimal amount of action is typically accomplished during this phase.

STAGE II. Different personalities and opinions, as well as struggles for control and power, can dominate at this stage, leading to infighting and competition among group members. As a team struggles to establish leadership and define tasks, tension may increase between members. Minimal work is accomplished at this stage of team development.

STAGE III. As teams move into this stage, they begin to establish rules for conducting and governing team activities and meetings. Group dynamics become more familiar, and team members begin to express

TEAM DEVELOPMENT CHART

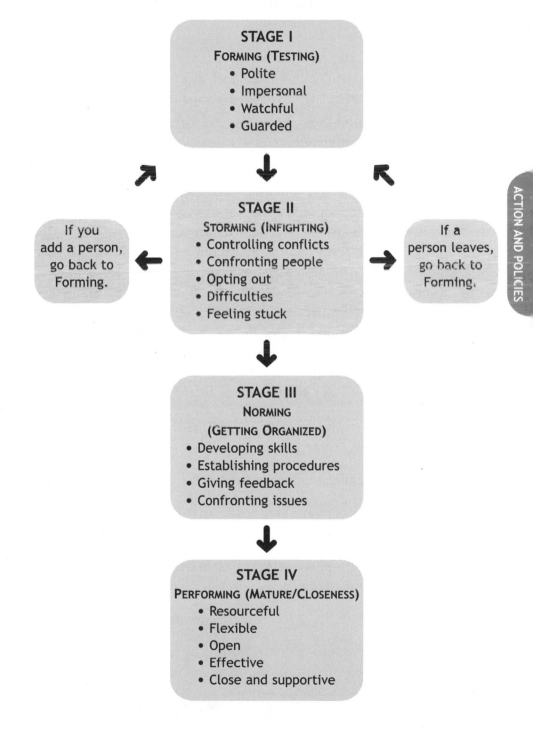

STAGE I
FORMING (TESTING)
- Polite
- Impersonal
- Watchful
- Guarded

if you add a person, go back to Forming.

STAGE II
STORMING (INFIGHTING)
- Controlling conflicts
- Confronting people
- Opting out
- Difficulties
- Feeling stuck

If a person leaves, go back to Forming.

STAGE III
NORMING
(GETTING ORGANIZED)
- Developing skills
- Establishing procedures
- Giving feedback
- Confronting issues

STAGE IV
PERFORMING (MATURE/CLOSENESS)
- Resourceful
- Flexible
- Open
- Effective
- Close and supportive

ACTION AND POLICIES

emotions and opinions more constructively, thereby accepting other team members and minimizing conflict. A moderate amount of action can be accomplished during this stage.

STAGE IV. After successfully navigating through the first three stages, teams are able to create a feeling of inclusiveness and respect. Team members can work together and are capable of diagnosing and solving problems and making decisions. The real work of the team is accomplished during this stage.

All of the stages are inevitable: the group works to build an atmosphere of trust in order to deal with issues and then move on to perform. The period of time spent in each stage, however, depends on leadership, the difficulty of the tasks involved, and the maturity of the group. To quickly move through Stage I and avoid becoming trapped in Stage II, a team should develop a mission together that is understood and accepted by all members. Each team member then should develop and work within a clear set of objectives and standards. This will help members understand the relationship between their individual objectives and the greater mission of the team. To develop a leadership community that demonstrates effective teamwork and group leadership, follow the guidelines below, which are adapted from *Parent Plus* (National PTA, 1995, p. 18).

The group should

- Have a clear understanding of its purpose and goals

- Be able to look forward and realize that means are inseparable from ends

- Provide an atmosphere in which members freely express their feelings and points of view

- Be able to initiate and carry out effective problem solving

- Be objective about its own functioning by recognizing the values and limitations of democratic methods and sticking to issues that are vital to its members

- Strike an appropriate balance between group productivity and the satisfaction of individual needs

- Make intelligent use of the differing abilities of its members

- Not be dominated by its leader or by any of its members, but have a high degree of cohesiveness and solidarity, allowing group members to share leadership responsibilities

See Appendix C for additional tools to help monitor a team's progress.

DEVELOPING A PARENT/FAMILY INVOLVEMENT POLICY

As an action team works to draft a parent/family involvement policy, it should seek input not only from team members, but also from groups and individuals within the community. Action teams should have regular and consistent access to other parents, so that they can knowledgeably represent the parents' views. Team members should also determine if their state's Department of Education has a state-level parent/family involvement policy to use as a model. The team should allow enough time for researching and evaluating current practices and for writing the policy to ensure a final product that truly fits the needs of the community and its families.

The policy should include a method for evaluation and revision. Teams should schedule community-wide hearings to allow for community reaction and comments on the final draft of the policy and follow the procedures of the school district to obtain school board support and adoption. (See Chapter 8 for techniques on forming partnerships with these groups.)

The policy should clearly communicate that parent involvement is an important strategy for increasing student success; therefore, all parent involvement plans and activities should be sensitive to the diversity of the school's population. The policy should also state that the board of education, district administration, and faculty are committed to helping develop and support school efforts to strengthen home-school partnerships. It is important to include this because administrators' and teachers' attitudes can determine how much and in what ways parents become involved in education.

An effective parent/family involvement policy should include elements that

- Encourage professional development for teachers and staff on how to communicate with parents

- Involve parents of children at all ages and grade levels in developing the policy

- Provide for outreach efforts to encourage participation of parents who may have low-level literacy skills or for whom English is not their primary language

- Recognize diverse family structures, circumstances, responsibilities, or differences that might present barriers to parent participation

- Inform parents regularly about education programs' objectives and their children's participation and progress in those programs

- Form links with special service agencies and community groups to address any family and community issues

- List components of successful home-school-community partnerships; the policy should refer to the National Standards and incorporate opportunities for parents to become involved in all the areas covered by the six National Standards

- Allow for opportunities for parents to participate in how parent/family involvement programs will be designed, implemented, assessed, and strengthened

A MODEL EXAMPLE: A SCHOOL SYSTEM IN PARTNERSHIP WITH THE PTA

In 1997 the Chicago School Reform Board of Trustees adopted a parent involvement policy at the 559 public schools in the Chicago Public

School System (CPS). The CPS is the third-largest school system in the country. Its policy, reprinted below, is based on the National Standards.

PARENT INVOLVEMENT RESOLUTION
Adopted by
The Chicago School Reform Board of Trustees
September 24, 1997
[97-0924-RS5]

WHEREAS, the goal of the Chicago Public Schools Children First Education Plan is "to assure Chicago's public school students will be well-prepared for the future: for work, further education and training, and family and civic responsibilities," and

WHEREAS, "central office management, principals, teachers, and parents share an unmatched dedication to improving student achievement," and

WHEREAS, findings from recent research cite:

"When parents are involved in their students' education, those students have higher grades and test scores, better attendance, and complete homework more consistently regardless of socioeconomic status, ethnic/racial background, or the parents' education level"; and

"Different types of parent/family involvement produce different gains. To have long-lasting gains for students, parent involvement activities must be well-planned, inclusive, and comprehensive at all grade levels."

NOW, THEREFORE, BE IT RESOLVED that the Chicago School Reform Board of Trustees supports the development, implementation, and regular evaluation of a parent involvement policy and program in every school which will involve parents at all grade levels in a variety of roles. The parent involvement programs will be comprehensive and coordinated in nature. They will include, but not be limited to, the following components of successful parent involvement programs:

- Regular, two-way, meaningful communication between home and school;

- Promotion and support of responsible parenting;

- Recognition that parents play an integral role in assisting student learning;

- A welcoming atmosphere for parents in the school and active solicitation of parents' support and assistance for school programs;

- Inclusion of parents as full partners in the decisions that affect children and families;

- Availability of community resources to strengthen school programs, family practices, and student learning.

The Board of Trustees supports professional development opportunities for all Chicago Public Schools staff members to enhance understanding of effective parent involvement strategies. The Board also recognizes the importance of administrative leadership in setting expectations and creating a climate conducive to parent participation.

In addition to programs at the schools, the Board supports the development, implementation, and regular evaluation of programs to involve parents in the decisions and practices of the school district, using to the degree possible the components listed above.

Engaging parents is essential to improved student achievement. The Chicago Public Schools fosters and supports active parent involvement.

—Reproduced with permission from the Office of
Communications, Chicago Public Schools

The PTA's Role

The Chicago Region PTA and the Illinois state PTA have been actively involved with the CPS system to help administrators, teachers, and parents learn the importance of parent involvement and to support the development of parent involvement programs. The Chicago Region PTA and the PTA advisory committee helped write and review the parent involvement resolution above. The advisory committee is a group of PTA representatives from schools across the system that serve as liaisons to the CPS to review policies, make recommendations, and help promote parent involvement. There are more than 22,600 parents in PTAs in 228 of Chicago's public schools (Chicago Public Schools, 1999, p. 31).

In October 1996, the Chicago Region PTA held a parent involvement summit to introduce the National Standards and begin to focus on parent involvement. This effort was supported by the National PTA, the CPS, and a national initiative funded by the Mattel Foundation called Hand in Hand: Parents, Schools, Communities United For Kids. After the Chicago Region resolution was created and adopted, the Chicago Region and Illinois state PTAs held a series of forums to introduce the resolution and the National Standards and begin to help educators, administrators, parents, and community members develop and evaluate parent involvement policies and programs based on the National Standards. More than 40% of the schools within the system participated in these forums. The Chicago Region PTA also held similar workshops for all six region education officers within the CPS system. Region education officers support local education initiatives, including the Local School Councils (LSCs) that are the local school governing bodies within the school system.

In May 1999, the Chicago Region PTA cooperated with the CPS to hold a citywide conference on parent involvement, entitled "Student Learning, a Family Affair." Open to anyone in a school community, such as parents, educators, and staff, the conference focused on the CPS parent involvement programs and other parent involvement programs, how parents can gain access to their schools, and how to improve communication and partnerships between parents, teachers, administrators, and the community. The Chicago Region PTA is currently providing

ACTION AND POLICIES

workshops to individual schools throughout the system on topics such as working with the community, working with the LSCs, and conducting parent-teacher conferences.

The School System's Role

Because policies need to be known to be effective, CPS administrators make an intensive effort to communicate its parent involvement policies. The Parent Involvement Resolution is sent to all principals each fall and has been shared with 300 outside organizations that work with the CPS in various ways.

The CPS has also created programs to implement the National Standards. Parents can volunteer through programs such as the Parent Attendance Officer Program, in which adults make sure students get to school safely every day in neighborhoods with a high incidence of crime. The CPS works with Chicago Cares to host an annual Serve-a-Thon day, in which families participate in hands-on volunteer projects such as painting school classrooms, lockers, and fences.

The CPS supports parenting through the Parent Resource and Support Center and through programs such as Helping Daily in School (HDIS), which provides parenting information and activities to develop leadership and parenting skills. The CPS supports parents as full partners in decision making by holding an average of four symposia a year to educate parents on issues such as curriculum, standards, school design, and discipline. In addition, nearly 4,500 parents and other citizens serve on LSCs throughout the city (Chicago Public Schools, 1999, p. 31). Local School Councils are responsible for a myriad of school governance issues, including principal selection and the evaluation of school budgets and improvement plans.

The CPS has formed partnerships with businesses to implement programs such as the Coca-Cola Valued Youth Program, which pairs 150 high school students as tutors and mentors with 300 elementary school children in an effort to prevent them from dropping out of school. This program has resulted in increased interest in school, better attendance, and improved academic performance in both groups.

The Coca-Cola Company's efforts to improve education through the Valued Youth Program and other programs were recognized with a Golden Star Award for Business Leadership in 1999. Sponsored by EdPress, this award recognizes the extraordinary efforts of a company to improve the quality of life through education, though its business lies mainly in other fields.

Through federal funding under the 21st Century Community Learning Centers Initiative, CPS established three full-service schools that remain open until 9:00 p.m. daily. These schools work directly with social service agencies to bring community resources into the school and provide after-school and weekend programs and activities for youths and adults.

The High School Reorganization Office is also trying to implement comprehensive parent involvement programs in Chicago's high schools by offering an orientation program for parents of freshmen to promote a more personal and proactive approach to involving parents at this level. In addition, some high schools are opening on Saturdays for community activities that involve parents and students.

IMPLEMENTING PARENT INVOLVEMENT POLICIES

If the goal is parent involvement, first develop policies that help enforce and define this goal, and then develop action plans that will help implement the policies. Action plans are important because parent involvement policies, even after they are adopted by the school district, cannot stand alone. To be effective, policies require thoughtful and comprehensive plans for their implementation. For example, the CPS has the LSCs and the PTA advisory committee to approve and monitor policy and improve plan implementation. Local schools should establish a permanent action team (i.e., a parent involvement committee or a site-based management team) to work with their school board to create a parent involvement policy and an action plan for its implementation, and then continually monitor and evaluate the process.

After the policies and action plans are supported by the board, they should be published in school newsletters and on school websites, along with information on what schools can do to support and ensure implementation of the policies. Ongoing training and professional development is essential to successful and long-lasting implementation.

Setting Goals and Developing Plans

As a team begins to create a policy and a plan for its implementation, it should also develop an appropriate set of goals. A goal is an optimistic view of what could be. A good goal statement is clearly written and contains a demand for action and planning that is easily measured. Goals should be simple statements that do not indicate how they might be achieved. Details on how to reach these goals should be included in a separate action plan, which is usually much more complex and longer.

In creating goals, teams should envision how these goals and their resulting policies would affect the school both now and in the future. Teams can identify long- and short-term goals by dividing team members into smaller groups to clarify, discuss, and write down suggestions for proposed goals. The small groups should then set priorities and submit three goals to the large group. The entire team can then further clarify, discuss, and prioritize these suggestions until both short- and long-term goals are established.

After the team establishes goals, it should develop action plans by considering the following questions:

- How can the team's vision be accomplished?

- What specific activities or projects will achieve the vision?

Teams can also use the ideas and forms here and in Appendix C to develop action plans. Action plans should

- Clarify the roles and responsibilities for all of the key players involved

- Address all goals developed

- Develop a time frame for accomplishing each goal

- Clarify what is needed to accomplish each goal

- Determine who will do what to accomplish each goal

- Designate how success will be evaluated

Action plans should also identify methods for initiating and ensuring parent involvement in all of the areas covered by the National Standards. See pages 183–184 for an example of a sample action plan. (See Appendix C for a blank copy.)

Action plans should be accompanied by a monthly planning calendar that incorporates how goals will be accomplished each month in all areas identified in the involvement policy and action plans. (See Appendix C for a monthly planning calendar.)

Evaluation

The action team should remain in place to help evaluate how well the new policies are being implemented in the school. Because an action team helps evenly distribute responsibilities and uses the skills, expertise, and experiences of many people, it is a good vehicle for evaluating how well the policies are being implemented. Original action team members can offer invaluable insight into how well policies are being implemented because they formulated the goals, policies, and action plans. For these reasons, it is important to keep team members interested in staying on the team for as long as possible. One way to do this is to acknowledge their work and offer ongoing support.

An effective team also needs to be open and flexible not just in its responsibilities, but also to outside evaluation of its work. Effective teams are willing to reorder the priority of activities, evaluate and revise timelines, and accept feedback from outside evaluators. For example, teams should regularly survey or hold meetings with families not immediately involved in the activities of the team to solicit their perspectives on how messages are being communicated and services are being received. Schools that have a partnership with a college or university could ask a student or instructor with an interest in parent/family issues to conduct an assessment of their progress. (See Appendix C for a sample form for assessing and evaluating a team's progress.)

For parent involvement in education to be meaningful, long-lasting, and effective, parent involvement policies, action plans, and activities must be well-planned, inclusive, and comprehensive. They must be routinely evaluated and revised based on the input of committed and motivated parents, community members, and an action team made up of local school community representatives.

ACTION PLAN FOR BUILDING
HOME-SCHOOL-COMMUNITY PARTNERSHIPS

(SAMPLE)

Area of Parent Involvement Focus:
Home-School-Community Communication

Activity: Develop a School Newsletter

Goals: 1. Inform parents/community of PTA/school activities
2. Provide opportunity for ongoing, two-way communication

ACTION AND POLICIES

What will be done?

Develop a newsletter with a professional layout and graphics that includes articles on school/PTA activities and timely parenting topics. Include a survey section in each newsletter for adults to complete and return or write in with questions. Post the newsletter on the school's website to provide access to members of the community.

Purpose of the activity

Provide information, resources, news, etc., to everyone in the school community; make information accessible to people in more than one way; and provide opportunities for community input and feedback.

Who will accomplish?

A committee of school staff, parents, teachers, a parent involvement professional or parent educator, community volunteers, and even students will write, edit, design, distribute, and post the newsletter online.

When?

The newsletter would be produced and distributed each month throughout the school year.

Evaluation: Evidence of success

The success of the newsletter could be determined by monitoring the interest shown in it, the number of times the newsletter web page is accessed, and the response to the survey section and parenting information published.

The action plan form is adapted from the original published in Parent Plus: A Comprehensive Program for Parent Involvement *(National PTA, 1995). See Appendix C for a blank action plan form.*

CHAPTER 10

TYING IT ALL TOGETHER

AFFIRMING THE SIGNIFICANCE OF PARENT AND FAMILY involvement has been one of the National PTA's priorities since its founding in 1897. During the past 100 years, the organization has consistently demonstrated that children benefit when parents and families are involved in education.

Because parent involvement can become the foundation upon which all other school reform is based, it is as important as the other areas in education for which national standards have been developed. National standards for parent involvement can improve parent involvement programs because they can be used to evaluate the quality and effectiveness of such programs nationwide.

The National PTA created the National Standards for Parent/Family Involvement Programs in 1997. Based on the research of Joyce Epstein of Johns Hopkins University, the standards were designed to help every school and program that serves children and families establish partnerships with parents and the community. These partnerships have the potential to increase parent involvement and use community resources to provide for the social, emotional, and academic growth and success of children.

EFFECTIVE PARENT INVOLVEMENT PROGRAMS

The most effective parent involvement programs will

1. Base their efforts on research

2. Implement the National Standards

3. Overcome barriers and reach out to key players

4. Develop action teams, parent involvement policies, and action plans

Base Efforts on Research

More than 85 research studies and the National PTA's many years of experience as advocates for children have shown that parent involvement increases student achievement and success. When parents are involved in their children's education, students are likely to do better in school regardless of their race or socioeconomic status (Henderson, 1987).

The most accurate predictors of student success are the family's ability, with the help and support of the school, to

1. Create a home environment that encourages learning

2. Communicate high yet reasonable expectations for their children's achievement and future careers

3. Become involved in their children's education at school and in the community (Henderson & Berla, 1995)

Overall, research indicates that school quality often improves when teachers and administrators have positive attitudes toward parents, actively encourage parent involvement, and design effective parent involvement programs (Lewis & Henderson, 1997).

Implement the National Standards

Parents play four key roles in successful, comprehensive, and inclusive parent involvement programs: teachers/nurturers, communicators/advisors, supporters/learners, and collaborators/decision makers. It is essential that schools support these roles, encourage parents to adopt them, and enable parents to be effective in each role.

The following six National Standards for Parent/Family Involvement Programs reflect and support these parenting roles:

- **COMMUNICATING**—Communication between home and school is regular, two-way, and meaningful.

- **PARENTING**—Parenting skills are promoted and supported.

- **STUDENT LEARNING**—Parents play an integral role in assisting student learning.

- **VOLUNTEERING**—Parents are welcome in the school, and their support and assistance are sought.

- **SCHOOL DECISION MAKING AND ADVOCACY**—Parents are full partners in the decisions that affect children and families.

- **COLLABORATING WITH THE COMMUNITY**—Community resources are used to strengthen schools, families, and student learning.

SUMMARY

The six program standards should be implemented together so that they have a synergistic effect, each multiplying the effects of the others. Together they are most effective and deliver their most powerful impact.

Overcome Barriers and Reach Out to Key Players

Research also shows that when it comes to parent involvement, the challenge is in transforming knowledge into practice and practice into results. Studies have shown that although most educators, administrators, and parents agree on the importance of parent involvement, efforts to involve parents in meaningful ways can fall short for two reasons: the failure to overcome barriers and the failure to reach out to key players.

OVERCOMING BARRIERS. It is not a lack of interest that keeps parents and families from being involved in their children's education. There are often genuine barriers blocking the way. Educators need to understand the various barriers to involvement and consider ways to respond to these barriers and meet the needs of parents.

ESTABLISHING PARTNERSHIPS WITH KEY PLAYERS. Everyone's involvement, support, and commitment is essential to establishing strong parent involvement programs that produce lasting results. Parent groups need to reach out to the key players in the school community and work together toward mutual goals. Leadership responsibilities need to extend beyond individual people and roles and be assumed by the school community as a whole. A good relationship between parent groups and the school's principal can pave the way for establishing partnerships between parents and teachers. Likewise, a strong partnership with the superintendent and local public officials can enhance relationships with parents and school board members.

Develop Action Teams, Parent Involvement Policies, and Action Plans

Developing parent involvement programs includes working to create a system for maintaining the momentum for real and lasting changes. To harness enthusiasm and energy and realize its goals, a school must form an action team that represents all concerned parties. The team has three responsibilities:

1. To develop a formal parent involvement policy

2. To develop action plans to implement the policy

3. To monitor and evaluate the implementation process

Action teams begin the process by examining the current parent involvement practices and setting long- and short-term goals for parent involvement initiatives. Once goals are established, action teams develop a policy on parent involvement and an action plan to implement the policy.

Both the policy and action plan should be based on the National Standards. The team should work with the superintendent and the school board to develop and ensure adoption of the policy and the action plans. After adoption, implementation begins. The team should regularly assess and evaluate the school's progress toward implementing the policy and improving its ability to meet the needs of families and the community.

BUILDING THE FUTURE

Building Successful Partnerships: A Guide for Developing Parent and Family Involvement Programs provides the information and tools for education communities to support meaningful parent and family participation in education, increase awareness of the components of effective parent involvement program design, and evaluate and improve current programs and practices. This nation's public schools help sustain our democratic society by expanding individual opportunity and providing an education to all children. We have a strong incentive to invest in the future—our children—and help them become productive citizens. With these goals in mind, the National PTA invites all teachers, administrators, and parent involvement professionals to support the National Standards for Parent/Family Involvement Programs. Working together, we can help today's students become tomorrow's leaders in school and in life.

SUMMARY

APPENDIXES

The position statement, surveys, forms, and worksheets in Appendixes A, B, and C may be reproduced and used in developing parent and family involvement programs. Permission to reprint these materials has been granted by the National PTA.

Full-size versions of the materials in Appendixes A, B, and C are also available in PDF (portable document format) on National PTA's website at http://www.pta.org/programs/bsp/.

NATIONAL PTA®
POSITION STATEMENT ON
PARENT/FAMILY INVOLVEMENT

NATIONAL PTA®
POSITION STATEMENT ON
PARENT/FAMILY INVOLVEMENT

PARENT/FAMILY INVOLVEMENT: EFFECTIVE PARENT INVOLVEMENT PROGRAMS TO FOSTER STUDENT SUCCESS

Parent involvement[1] is the participation of parents in every facet of the education and development of children from birth to adulthood. Parent involvement takes many forms, including parents as first educators; as decision makers about children's education, health, and well-being; as well as advocates for children's success. It is recognized that parents are the primary influence in their children's lives.

FAMILY'S CONTRIBUTIONS

National PTA recognizes the research that demonstrates when parents are involved, students achieve more, regardless of socioeconomic status, ethnic/racial background, or the parents' education level. The most accurate predictor of a student's achievement in school is not income or social status, but the extent to which that student's family is able to

- create a home environment that encourages learning and nurtures their children's physical, mental, social, and spiritual education

---

[1]National PTA recognizes that other adults may carry the primary responsibility for a child's education, development, and well-being. Therefore, all references to "parent" involvement include any primary caregiver or adult who plays an important role in a child's family life.

- communicate high, yet reasonable, expectations for their children's achievement and future careers

- develop knowledge of how their children function in the school environment by becoming involved in their children's education at school and in the community

This involvement is essential for the positive emotional and social development, cultural growth, and academic achievement of every child.

SCHOOL'S CONTRIBUTIONS

Parent involvement programs should match the needs of the school, students, parents, and the community. Goal 8 of the National Education Goals states, "Every school will promote partnerships that will increase parental involvement and participation in promoting the social, emotional, and academic growth of children." Schools and other programs will

- design comprehensive strategies to bring together all of the stakeholders by building partnerships among all of the major groups in the school community

- share accurate information about the school's goals, programs, and policies in languages that are accessible to all partners

- know, interact with, and involve stakeholders in all stages of program planning, design, and implementation

SCHOOL-FAMILY-COMMUNITY PARTNERSHIPS

Truly comprehensive programs result in effective schools that will ensure that communication between home and school is regular, two-way, and meaningful. These programs will do the following:

- promote and support parenting skills

- allow parents to play an integral role in assisting student learning

- welcome parents in the school and seek their support and assistance

- ensure parents are full partners in the decisions affecting children and families

- encourage collaboration with the community

ORGANIZATION'S CONTRIBUTIONS

The task of connecting families and schools is both formidable and attainable. Affirming the significance of parent and family involvement has been a priority of National PTA since its founding in 1897. PTA must function as an independent, nonpartisan, child advocacy group that reflects the community's collaborative aspirations for all children. To protect the education, health, and well-being of all children, PTA has a responsibility to

- advocate for and support legislation that promotes meaningful parent involvement

- assure access to an equitable and quality education for all children

- ensure that children have the support necessary in the home, school, and community

- seek information on policies, curriculum, and laws that affect children

- share accurate information about educational goals, programs, and progress with parents and the public

- know, support, and interact with students, teachers, administrators, and community

- be willing to accept responsibility for the vitality of PTA to assure an active PTA

- work within the PTA and the school in a constructive manner with respect for democratic procedures and a tolerance for a diversity of opinion

- participate in decisions affecting school goals, policies, programs, curriculum materials, rules, and regulations

- increase opportunities for the development of parenting skills and promote training to develop child advocates

Adopted in 1991 by the National PTA Board of Directors

Revised in 1999 by the National PTA Board of Directors

Reviewed by the 1993 and 1996 National PTA Convention Resolutions Committee

Appendix B

SURVEYS

PARENT INVOLVEMENT IN OUR SCHOOLS

For the purposes of this survey, I am responding as a(n):

❑ parent   ❑ teacher   ❑ administrator   ❑ other: _____

Some of these questions are deliberately intended to expose differences of opinions between parents and school professionals. The survey is not intended to be an end in itself, but rather to serve as a means for opening up a dialogue between the two groups.

Section 1: Respond to the following statements by checking "Yes" or "No."

1. There should be many school activities that involve students, parents, and teachers, such as reading enrichment programs, sports events, and recognition ceremonies to honor student achievement. ❑ Yes ❑ No

2. Parents should be encouraged to work in the school as volunteers. ❑ Yes ❑ No

3. Parents should supervise children with homework. ❑ Yes ❑ No

4. Parents should be able to schedule visits to the school during the day to understand the kinds of experiences their child is having in school. ❑ Yes ❑ No

5. There should be parent education classes run by the PTA, in cooperation with resource personnel provided by the school, to teach parents how to help their children benefit from school. ❑ Yes ❑ No

6. Parents' primary connection with the school should be to sponsor activities such as potluck suppers, fund-raising activities, open houses, and the like. ❑ Yes ❑ No

7. Parents should initiate personal conferences with teachers when they feel it is necessary (outside of regularly scheduled parent-teacher conferences). ❑ Yes ❑ No

8. Parents should attend school board meetings. ❑ Yes ❑ No

Section 2: Please respond to each statement by circling the number that comes closest to your thoughts about the appropriate level of parent involvement.

Ratings: 3 = Parents should be actively involved throughout this process.

2 = Parents should be asked for input before education professionals plan programs or set policies.

1 = Parents should be asked to review revised programs and policies.

0 = Not an appropriate role for parents—should be left solely to education professionals.

1. Developing written school district policies (such as attendance, homework, and graduation requirements) 0 1 2 3

2. Developing written goals for increasing parent involvement 0 1 2 3

3. Planning written goals for increasing parent involvement 0 1 2 3

4. Deciding/evaluating how well teachers and principals do their jobs and how to reward and retain good teachers 0 1 2 3

5. Determining policy on when students should be held back rather than promoted to the next grade 0 1 2 3

6. Setting up a school advisory group to bring suggestions for changes to the principal and school board 0 1 2 3

7. Establishing the discipline code in the school 0 1 2 3

8. Selecting textbooks and other learning materials 0 1 2 3

9. Developing the school budget 0 1 2 3

10. Serving on the team that revises report cards   0   1   2   3

11. Participating in school events such as parties,
    field trips, sports events, plays, etc.   0   1   2   3

12. Establishing a policy for recognizing outstanding
    teacher performance   0   1   2   3

Section 3: Please answer the following question.

The PTA program in our school should be (check one):

❑ expanded   ❑ maintained   ❑ reduced

Comments:

_____

_____

_____

WHAT THE ANSWERS AND SCORES MEAN

Section 1: Answers

If you responded as a parent:
The more "yes" answers you circled (with the exception of question 6), the more you value parent involvement in education and believe that parents have an important role in the school environment.

If you responded as a teacher or as an administrator:
The more "yes" answers you circled (with the exception of number 6), the more open you are to including parents in the education process and having them play a visible role at the school.

Section 2: Scores

If you responded as a parent:
The lower the number circled in Section 2 the more you believe the schools should handle education decisions. You are unsure of the appropriateness of parents becoming involved as cooperative partners with school professionals. The higher your score, the more you want to help make school decisions on behalf of your own and all children in the community. You are highly motivated and want to empower other parents to be meaningfully involved.

APPENDIXES

If you responded as a teacher or as an administrator:
The lower the number circled in Section 2, the more you question the value of parent involvement in education. The higher your score, the more open you are to including parents in education planning. You are receptive to trying new ideas because the ultimate beneficiaries are the children. You have an easy relationship with parents in your community, and they ask your opinions and trust your judgment.

Source: The National Standards for Parent/Family Involvement Programs Training Module, National PTA, 1998.

PARENT SURVEY

The PTA needs your help to plan parent involvement programs at our school. Parent involvement is fun, informative, and most important of all, it helps our children perform better in school. Please take a few minutes to fill out this survey and return it to:

_____

_____

1. What specifically would you like to know about the school?

    _____

    _____

2. **From what sources do you get most of your information about school? (Check one)**

    ❏ Newsletter ❏ Friends

    ❏ Children ❏ Newspaper

    ❏ Teachers ❏ TV

    ❏ Principal ❏ Other _____

3. **Would you be interested in attending a class or session on how parents can help their children learn at home?**

    ❏ Yes ❏ No

4. **If you checked "yes" for question 3, please indicate below the types of workshops you would like to participate in to help you help your children learn.**

   ❏ Helping with homework

   ❏ Improving reading skills

   ❏ Improving math skills

   ❏ Testing programs and what they mean

   ❏ English as a second language

   ❏ Improving your child's self-image

   ❏ Building your own parenting skills

   ❏ Helping your child explore career choices

   ❏ Saying no to drugs

   ❏ Explaining HIV/AIDS and steps to protect your child

   ❏ Recognizing gang symbols and activities

   ❏ Other _____

5. **Where would you like these parenting programs to be held?**

   ❏ In the school

   ❏ In a community/public facility

   ❏ In the home of a parent in your neighborhood or area

   Would you be willing to host such a session?

   ❏ Yes   ❏ No

6. **When would you like to have these meetings scheduled?**

   ❏ On a week night

   ❏ In the early morning before school starts

   ❏ Some time during a weekday
      ❏ Morning   ❏ Afternoon

   ❏ On a Saturday
      ❏ Morning   ❏ Afternoon   ❏ Evening

   ❏ On a Sunday
      ❏ Morning   ❏ Afternoon   ❏ Evening

7. **Would you be interested in participating in a small-group cof-fee discussion hour at the school?**

   ❏ Yes   ❏ No
   　Best time: ❏ Morning   ❏ Afternoon   ❏ Evening

8. **Do you agree with the following statements:**

   I can talk openly with my child's teacher(s).

   ❏ Yes   ❏ No   ❏ To some degree

   I can talk openly with my child's principal.

   ❏ Yes   ❏ No   ❏ To some degree

   I am well-informed by the school or teachers about what my child is doing at school.

   ❏ Yes   ❏ No   ❏ To some degree

   I feel that teachers need to be aware of home problems that may affect my child's work.

   ❏ Yes   ❏ No   ❏ To some degree

9. **How effective are the following toward improving communica-tions between your family and the school?**

	Good	Fair	Poor
Open houses	❏	❏	❏
Grade-level orientation sessions	❏	❏	❏
Parent-teacher conferences	❏	❏	❏
PTA meetings	❏	❏	❏
School/PTA newsletter	❏	❏	❏

APPENDIXES

10. **As a parent, do you have trouble with any of the following?**

	Yes	No	To some degree
Your child's homework	❑	❑	❑
Attending school functions	❑	❑	❑
Spending enough time with your child	❑	❑	❑
Getting in to see your child's teacher(s)	❑	❑	❑
Dealing with your child's problems	❑	❑	❑
Knowing school policies	❑	❑	❑
Motivating your child	❑	❑	❑

11. **Would you like to volunteer in the following areas?**

	Yes	No
Clerical or administrative duties for school or PTA	❑	❑
Helping in your child's classroom (reading aloud, working with individual students, etc.)	❑	❑
Organizing a PTA or school event (open house, holiday program, cultural arts fair, etc.)	❑	❑
Supervising student events or field trips	❑	❑
Participating on an advisory committee (on curriculum and textbooks, for example)	❑	❑
Talking to students about careers or hobbies	❑	❑

Other _____

12. **Check the kinds of resources and services you would like to see made available at the school.**

❑ Homework hotline

❑ Before- or after-school child care

❑ Parent resource center

❑ Parent support group

❑ Family use of gym, pool, or school library

❑ Other _____

13. I have the following hobbies and work experience that I would be willing to share with the students, school, or PTA:

_____

_____

_____

_____

14. Parent and family involvement at school should be strengthened in the following ways:

_____

_____

_____

_____

Optional (please complete if you responded positively to questions 11 or 13):

Name _____

Address _____

Best time to contact _____

Phone _____

E-mail _____

Source: The National Standards for Parent/Family Involvement Programs Training Module, National PTA, 1998.

FACULTY SURVEY

Dear Faculty Member:

The PTA is developing ways to encourage family and community support of our schools. The information you provide will help us better serve the entire school community. Please take a few minutes to fill out this survey and return it to:

PTA contact: _____

1. Do you currently have parents or other family members volunteering in your classroom or for other activities?

   ❑ Yes   ❑ No

2. Would you consider using parents/community volunteers in your classroom?

   ❑ Yes   ❑ No

   If no, why not? _____

   _____

   _____

3. What are your current needs for assistance?

   ❑ Materials   ❑ Visual aids
   ❑ Books and magazines   ❑ Other
   ❑ Art supplies   (Question continues on next page.)

3. **What are your current needs for assistance? (continued)**

❑ Volunteers to help with the following:

❑ Support tasks, e.g., gather resources; set up learning centers, displays, or experiments; arrange for speakers or field trips; record tapes for learning centers

❑ One-on-one teaching tasks
    ❑ Listen to a child read
    ❑ Coach in spelling or math facts
    ❑ Practice vocabulary with non-English-speaking students
    ❑ Other _____

❑ Small-group or class teaching tasks
    ❑ Perform or help with music
    ❑ Supervise parties or field trips
    ❑ Talk to students about careers or hobbies
    ❑ Other _____

4. **What areas do you feel the PTA needs to address?**

    _____
    _____
    _____

5. **What methods have you found effective for improving home-school communications (phone calls, newsletters, notes, etc.)?**

    _____
    _____
    _____

Optional

Your name _____
Best time to contact _____
Grade(s) _____
Subject(s) _____

Source: The National Standards for Parent/Family Involvement Programs Training Module, National PTA, 1998.

Appendix C

FORMS AND WORKSHEETS

EVALUATING GROUP PROCESS

To analyze the progress of your team, have each member independent-
ly rate each variable on a scale of 1 to 5. *Adopted from National PTA
Leadership Materials.*

1 = missing completely ⟶ 5 = operating ideally

1. Listening: Members don't
really listen to one another,
they interrupt and don't try to
understand others.

1 2 3 4 5

All members really listen and
try to understand others.

2. Open Communication:
Members are guarded or
cautious in discussion.

1 2 3 4 5

Members express both
thoughts and feelings openly.

**3. Mutual Trust and
Confidence:** Members show
suspicion of one another's
motives.

1 2 3 4 5

Members trust one another
and do not fear ridicule or
reprisal.

**4. Attitudes Toward
Differences Within Group:**
Members avoid argument,
smooth differences, suppress or
avoid conflicts.

1 2 3 4 5

Members search for, respect,
and accept differences and
work through them openly;
they are not pressured to
conform.

5. Problem Solving: When
disagreements occur members
are not able to initiate and
conduct effective problem
solving.

1 2 3 4 5

Members are able to address
differences and solve
problems in positive and
proactive ways.

6. Mutual Support: Members are defensive about themselves and their functions.

1 2 3 4 5

Members are able to give and receive help.

7. Involvement/Participation: A few members dominate discussion.

1 2 3 4 5

All members are involved, free to participate in any way.

8. Control Methods: The chair controls subject matter and decisions.

1 2 3 4 5

All members accept responsibility for productive discussion and for decisions.

9. Flexibility: The group is locked in on established rules, and members find it hard to change or revise procedures.

1 2 3 4 5

Members readily change procedures in response to new situations.

10. Use of Member's Resources: Individual's knowledge, abilities, and experience are not used.

1 2 3 4 5

Each member's knowledge, abilities, and experience are fully used.

11. Objectives and Purposes: Objectives and goals are not clear or not understood and there is no commitment to them.

1 2 3 4 5

Objectives are clear, understood, and there is full commitment to them.

12. Vision: Members are not able to look and plan ahead to realize their long-term goals.

1 2 3 4 5

Members can see that the means are inseparable from the ends and can plan ahead to meet their goals.

(Survey from *Parent Plus: A Comprehensive Program for Parent Involvement*, National PTA, 1995)

ACTION PLAN FOR BUILDING HOME-SCHOOL-COMMUNITY PARTNERSHIPS

Area of Parent Involvement Focus: _____

Activity: _____

Goal: _____

What will be done?
Purpose of the activity
Who will accomplish?

When?

Resources/materials needed

Training needs

Evaluation: Evidence of success

(Action Plan adapted from the original published in *Parent Plus: A Comprehensive Program for Parent Involvement,* National PTA, 1995)

PLANNING CALENDAR

Month:_____

Activities in parent involvement that support the National Standards for Parent/Family Involvement Programs

---

I. Communicating: Activities that promote communication between home and school that is two-way, regular and meaningful

II. Parenting: Activities that promote and support parenting skills

III. Student Learning: Activities that support parents playing an integral role in student's learning

IV. Volunteering: Activities that welcome parents and support their assistance

V. School Decision Making and Advocacy: Activities that support parents as full partners in decision making with the school

VI. Collaborating with Community: Activities that promote community resources being used to strengthen schools, families, and student learning

EVALUATING PTA PARENT/FAMILY INVOLVEMENT ACTIVITIES

The chart on page 222 is designed to help you evaluate your PTA parent/family involvement activities. List PTA/school activities and events that you conducted during the month. Distribute this form to parents, teachers, students, and community members to complete and return.

In each square, ask participants to put + for above average, 0 for average, - for below average, or N/A for not applicable (as to how each activity supports and meets the criteria).

EVALUATING PTA PARENT/FAMILY INVOLVEMENT ACTIVITIES

Directions: In each square, put **+** for above average, **0** for average, **-** for below average, or N/A for not applicable (as to how each activity supports and meets the criteria).

Criteria for Activities	Activities/Events		
Home-school communication			
Parenting skills			
Parents as partners in decision making			
Parents as advocates			
Parents as volunteers			
Parents as educators in the home			
Uses community resources			
Outreach to parents and community			
Promotes positive action/activity			
Clear in its purpose			
Meets parents' needs			
Involves school personnel			
Involves teachers and administrators			
Benefits children's education			

(Evaluation Chart adapted from the original published in *Parent Plus: A Comprehensive Program for Parent Involvement,* National PTA, 1995)

Appendix D

RESOURCES

RESOURCES

GETTING ON BOARD

Ordering the National Standards

The National Standards offer a research-based framework and field-tested strategies that enable schools to organize effective school-family-community partnerships. These standards are making parent involvement integral to the work of many local, state, and national education organizations. Since their introduction, the National Standards for Parent/Family Involvement Programs have been adopted in schools and school districts across the county and endorsed by nearly 50 national organizations. The content of the National Standards booklet is available on the National PTA's website at www.pta.org. The National Standards booklet can also be ordered from the National Educational Service. For details, contact NES by e-mail at nes@nesonline.com or call (800) 733-6786.

National PTA Cooperating Organizations

More than 40 national education, health, and parent involvement organizations have endorsed or support the National Standards for Parent/Family Involvement Programs. National PTA thanks the following organizations and institutions for agreeing to uphold these standards.

Organizations marked with an asterisk (*) are partners in the **Learning First Alliance** (LFA), an organization composed of 12 leading national education associations, including the National PTA. These leaders in education work together strategically and aggressively to improve student learning in America's public elementary and secondary schools. For more information, contact

Learning First Alliance
1001 Connecticut Avenue N.W.
Suite 335
Washington, DC 20036
(202) 296-5220
www.learningfirst.org

Academy for Educational Development
1825 Connecticut Avenue N.W.
Washington, DC 20009
(202) 884-8000, www.aed.org

American Academy of Pediatrics
141 Northwest Place Boulevard
Elk Grove Village, IL 60007-1098
(847) 981-7396, www.aap.org

*American Association of Colleges for Teacher Education
1307 New York Avenue N.W., Suite 300
Washington, DC 20005-4701
(202) 293-2450, www.aacte.org

*American Association of School Administrators
Leadership for Learning Foundation
1801 North Moore Street
Arlington, VA 22209
(703) 528-0700, www.aasa.org

*American Federation of Teachers
555 New Jersey Avenue N.W.
Washington, DC 20001
(202) 879-4400, www.aft.org

American School Counselor Association
801 North Fairfax Street, Suite 310
Alexandria, VA 22314
(800) 306-4722, (703) 683-2722, www.schoolcounselor.org

American School Health Association
7263 State Route 43, P.O. Box 708
Kent, OH 44240
(330) 678-1601, www.ashaweb.org

The ASPIRA Association Inc.
1444 I Street N.W., Suite 800
Washington, DC 20005
(202) 835-3600, www.aspira.org

***Association for Supervision and Curriculum Development**
1703 North Beauregard Street
Alexandria, VA 22311-1714
(703) 578-9600, (800) 933-ASCD, www.ascd.org

Association of State and Territorial Health Officials
1275 K Street N.W., Suite 800
Washington, DC 20005-4006
(202) 371-9090

Center for Law and Education
1875 Connecticut Avenue N.W., Suite 510
Washington, DC 20009
(202) 986-3000, www.cleweb.org

Center on School, Family, and Community Partnerships
Johns Hopkins University
3505 North Charles Street, Suite 200
Baltimore, MD 21218
(410) 516-8800, www.csos.jhu.edu

Communities In Schools of Georgia
1252 West Peachtree Street, Suite 430
Atlanta, GA 30309
(800) 838-5784, (404) 888-5784, www.cisga.org

Community Solutions International
1222 Hemlock Street N.W.
Washington, DC 20012
(202) 882-2182

Corporation for Educational Technology
238 S. Meridian Street, 4th Floor
Indianapolis, IN 46225
(317) 687-6059, www.buddyproject.org

Council for Exceptional Children
1920 Association Drive
Reston, VA 20191-1589
(703) 620-3660, www.cec.sped.org

*Council of Chief State School Officers
One Massachusetts Avenue N.W., Suite 700
Washington, DC 20001-1431
(202) 408-5505, www.ccsso.org

Council of the Great City Schools
1301 Pennsylvania Avenue, Suite 702
Washington, DC 20004
(202) 393-2427, www.cgcs.org

Family Education Network
Statler Building, Suite 1215
20 Park Plaza
Boston, MA 02116
(617) 542-6500, www.familyeducation.com

Family Impact Seminar
1730 Rhode Island Avenue N.W., Suite 209
Washington, DC 20036
(301) 656-9666

Howard University Graduate Programs in Urban School Psychology/
School of Education
2400 6th Street N.W.
Washington, DC 20059
(202) 806-6100, FAX (202) 806-7018, www.howard.edu

Megaskills Education Center of the Home and School Institute
1500 Massachusetts Avenue N.W.
Washington, DC 20005
(202) 466-3633, www.megaskillshsi.org

*National Association of Elementary School Principals
1615 Duke Street
Alexandria, VA 22314
(800) 39-NAESP, (703) 684-3345, www.naesp.org

National Association of Partners in Education
901 North Pitt Street, Suite 320
Alexandria, VA 22314
(703) 836-4880, www.nape.org

National Association of School Nurses
P.O. Box 1300
Scarborough, ME 04070-1300
(207) 883-2117, www.nash.org

National Association of School Psychologists
     4340 East West Highway, Suite 402
     Bethesda, MD 20814
     (301) 657-0270, www.naspweb.org

*National Association of Secondary School Principals
     1904 Association Drive
     Reston, VA 20190-1537
     (703) 860-0200, www.nasp.org

National Association of State Directors of Vocational Technical Education
     Consortium
     444 North Capitol Street N.W.
     Washington, DC 20001
     (202) 737-0303, www.iris.org/~nasdvtec

National Coalition of Title I/Chapter I Parents
     1541 14th Street N.W.
     Washington, DC 20005
     (202) 547 9286

National Council for Accreditation of Teacher Education
     2010 Massachusetts Avenue, N.W., Suite 500
     Washington, DC 20036-1023
     (202) 466-7496, www.ncate.org

National Council of La Raza
     1111 19th Street N.W., Suite 1000
     Washington, DC 20036
     (202) 785-1670, www.nclr.org

National Dropout Prevention Center
     Clemson University
     209 Martin Street
     Clemson, SC 29631-1555
     (864) 656-2599, www.dropoutprevention.org

*National Education Association
     1201 16th Street N.W.
     Washington, DC 20036
     (202) 833-4000, www.nea.org

National Head Start Association
     1651 Prince Street
     Alexandria, VA 22314
     (703) 739-0875, www.nhsa.org

APPENDIXES

National Information Center for Children and Youth with Disabilities
P.O. Box 1492
Washington, DC 20013-1492
(800) 695-0285 voice/TTY, (202) 884-8200 voice/TTY,
www.nichcy.org

National Middle School Association
4151 Executive Parkway, Suite 300
Westerville, OH 43081
(800) 528-6672, www.nmsa.org

*National Parent Teacher Association
330 N. Wabash Avenue, Suite 2100
Chicago, IL 60611-3690
(800) 307-4PTA (4782), (312) 670-6782, www.pta.org

*National School Boards Association
1680 Duke Street
Alexandria, VA 22314-3493
(703) 838-6700, www.nsba.org

National Urban League
120 Wall Street
New York, NY 10005
(212) 558-5300, www.nul.org

Parents as Teachers National Center, Inc.
9374 Olive Boulevard, Suite 230
St. Louis, MO 63132
(314) 432-4330, www.patnc.org

Project Parents Inc.
24 Appleton Street
Boston, MA 02116
(617) 451-0360, www.projectparents.org

School Improvement Council Assistance
University of South Carolina
Columbia, SC 29208
(803) 777-7658, www.ed.sc.edu/sica/sica.html

Websters International
240 Wilson Pike Circle
Brentwood, TN 37027
(615) 373-1723, www.bowdoinmethod.com

BIBLIOGRAPHY

American Association of School Administrators. (1999). *Preparing schools and school systems for the 21st century.* Arlington, VA: Author.

Baker, A. (1996). *Parents as school partners.* New York: National Council of Jewish Women, Center for the Child.

Baskwill, J. (1989). *Parents and teachers: Partners in learning.* New York: Scholastic.

Brimhall, D., West, J., & Winquist-Nord, C. (1997). *Fathers' involvement in their children's schools.* Washington, DC: National Center for Education Statistics, U.S. Department of Education.

Bryson, K., & Casper, L. (1998). *Current population reports—Household and family characteristics: March 1997.* Washington, DC: U.S. Bureau of the Census.

Campbell-Lehn, C. (1997). Assumptions create barriers to school volunteer success. *The Journal of Volunteer Administration, 25*(2), 8–15.

Campbell-Lehn, C. (1998). Finding the right fit: Creating successful volunteer job descriptions. *The Journal of Volunteer Administration, 26*(3), 22–29.

Cavarretta, J. (1998, May) PARENTS are a SCHOOL'S BEST FRIEND. *Educational Leadership,* 55, 12–15.

Chandler, K., & Vaden-Kiernan, N. (1996). *Parents' reports of school practices to involve families.* Washington, DC: National Center for Education Statistics, U.S. Department of Education.

Chang, H., Salazar, D., & Leong, C. (1994). *Drawing strengths from diversity: Effective services for children, youth and families.* San Francisco: California Tomorrow.

Chavkin, N. (1998). Making the case for school, family and community partnerships: Recommendations for research. *The School Community Journal, 8*(1), 9–21.

Chicago Public Schools. (1999). *Public schools trending up: Three-year education progress report.* Chicago: Author.

Christopher, C. J. (1996). *Building parent-teacher communication: An educator's guide.* Lancaster, PA: Technomic.

The Conference Board. (1997). *A business guide to support employee and family involvement in education.* New York: Author.

Education Week. (1999, January 11). Quality counts '99: Rewarding results, punishing failure. Special report issue of *Education Week, 18*(17), 1–206.

Epstein, J. L. (1995, May). School, family, community partnerships: Caring for the children we share. *Phi Delta Kappa, 77,* 701–712.

Epstein, J. L., & Clark-Salinas, K. (1997). *Manual for teachers and prototype activities: Teachers involve parents in schoolwork (TIPS) language arts, science/health, and math interactive homework in the elementary grades/middle grades, and prototype activities.* Baltimore: Center on School, Family, and Community Partnerships, Johns Hopkins University.

Epstein, J. L., & Dauber, S. L. (1991). School programs and teacher practice of parent involvement in inner-city elementary and middle schools. *The Elementary School Journal, 91*(3), 289–305.

Epstein J. L., & Lee, S. (1995). National patterns of school and family connections in the middle grades. In B. Ryan, G. Adams, T. Gullotta, R. Weissberg, & R. Hampton (Eds.), *Family-school connection: Theory, research, and practice,* 289–305. Thousand Oaks, CA: Sage.

Epstein, J. L., Coates, L., Clark-Salinas, K., Sanders, M. G., & Simon, B. (1997). *Partnership 2000 schools manual: Improving school-family community connections.* Baltimore: Johns Hopkins University.

Galinsky, E., Colmenares, M., Goldsmith, J., Hardman, R., Haskell, T., Otterbourg, S., & Vosburgh, L. (1995). *Employers, families and education.* Washington, DC: Partnership for Family Involvement in Education, U.S. Department of Education.

Gary, W., Barbara, H., Marburger, C. L., & Witherspoon, R. (1996). *Family, school, and community partnerships.* Washington, DC: National Education Association.

Great Lakes Resource Access Project. (1991, December). *Successful volunteer systems, 2*(3).

Hatch, T. (1998, May). How community action contributes to achievement. *Educational Leadership, 55,* 16–19.

Henderson, A. T. (1987). *The evidence continues to grow.* Columbia, MD: National Committee for Citizens in Education.

Henderson, A. T., & Berla, N. (1981). *The evidence grows.* Washington, DC: Center for Law and Education.

Henderson, A. T., & Berla, N. (1995). *A new generation of evidence: The family is critical to student achievement.* Washington, DC: Center for Law and Education.

Henderson, A. T., Jones, K., & Raimondo, B. (1999, April). The power of parent partnership. *Our Children, 24,* 36–37.

Kellaghan, T., Sloane, K., Alvarez, B., & Bloom, B. (1993). *The home environment and school learning: Promoting parental involvement in the education of children.* San Francisco: Jossey-Bass.

Kibel B., & Stein-Seroussi, A. (1997). *Effective community mobilization: Lessons from experience.* Rockville, MD: U.S. Department of Health and Human Services, Center for Substance Abuse Prevention.

Klumpp, K. (1990). *Barriers to successful outreach to parents of diverse populations.* San Diego, CA: San Diego PTA Unified Council's Project Hope.

Lambert, L. (1998). *Building leadership capacity in schools.* Alexandria, VA: Association for Supervision and Curriculum Development.

Leithwood, K., & Menzies, T. (1998). Forms and effects of school-based management: A review. *Educational Policy, 12,* 325–346.

Lewis, A. C., & Henderson, A. T. (1997). *Urgent message: Families crucial to school reform.* Washington, DC: Center for Law and Education.

Lewis, A. C., & Henderson, A. T. (1999). *Urgent message for parents.* Washington, DC: Center for Law and Education.

Lueder, D. C. (1998). *Creating partnerships with parents: An educator's guide.* Lancaster, PA: Technomic.

National Center for Education Statistics. (1998). *Parent involvement in children's education: Efforts by public elementary schools.* Washington, DC: U.S. Department of Education.

National Education Goals Panel. (1998). *The national education goals report: Executive summary: Improving education through family-school-community partnerships.* Washington, DC: Author.

National PTA. (1995). *Parent plus: A comprehensive program for parent involvement.* Chicago: Author.

National PTA. (1998a). *National standards for parent/family involvement programs.* Chicago: Author.

National PTA. (1998b). *Parents on public education: National survey of parents of public school students.* Washington, DC: Bennett, Petts and Blumenthal. (Published on National PTA's website at http://www.pta.org/programs/parentsur/index.htm.)

National PTA & World Book. (1993). *World book survey of elementary school parents.* Elk Grove Village, IL: World Book Educational Products.

National PTA, National Association of Elementary School Principals, & World Book. (1991). *The little things make a big difference: How to help your children succeed in school.* Elk Grove Village, IL: World Book Educational Products.

National School Public Relations Association. (1991, September). Communication is a key: Effective parenting skills can be learned. *IT STARTS in the Classroom, 8.*

Neal, R. (1991). *School-based management: A detailed guide for successful implementation.* Bloomington, IN: National Educational Service.

Newsweek Inc., Chrysler, & the National PTA. (1990). *Education in America: Getting the nation involved.* New York: Newsweek Inc.

Newsweek Inc., Chrysler, & the National PTA. (1991). *Second annual survey on parental involvement in education.* New York: Newsweek Inc.

Newsweek Inc., Chrysler, and the National PTA. (1993). *The third PTA national educational study: A study of attitudes and behavior regarding children's education.* New York: Newsweek Inc.

Office of Educational Research and Improvement. (1998). *Helping your students with homework: A guide for teachers.* Washington, DC: U.S. Department of Education.

Ogawa, R., & White, P. (1994). School-based management: An overview. In S. A. Mohrman (Ed.), *School-based management: Organizing for high performance,* (pp. 53–80). San Francisco: Jossey-Bass.

Palm, R., & Toma, D. (1997, Fall). Community relationships and partnerships. *New Directions for Student Services, 79,* 57–65.

Public Agenda. (1999). *Playing their parts: Parents and teachers talk about parental involvement in public schools.* New York: Author.

Sarason, S. (1995). *Parent involvement and the political principle: Why the existing governance structure of schools should be abolished.* San Francisco: Jossey-Bass.

Stinson, J. F. (1997, March). New data on multiple jobholding available from the CPS. *Monthly Labor Review,* 3–8.

U.S. Census Bureau. (1997). Census brief: Children with single parents—how they fare. Washington, DC: Author.

U.S. Department of Education. (1994). *Strong families, strong schools.* Washington, DC: Author.

U.S. Department of Education. (1996). *Reaching all families: Creating family-friendly schools.* Washington, DC: Author.

U.S. Department of Education. (1997). *Overcoming barriers to family involvement in Title I schools.* Washington, DC: Author.

White-Clark, R., Decker, L., & Mott, C. (1996). The "hard-to-reach" parent: Old challenges, new insights. Boca Raton, FL: Florida Atlantic University.

Wisconsin Department of Public Instruction. (1993). *Volunteer-a-Thon: At the heart of change,* Madison, WI: Author.

ABOUT THE AUTHOR:
NATIONAL PTA®

NATIONAL PTA IS THE OLDEST AND LARGEST volunteer child advocacy association in the United States working exclusively on behalf of children and youth. In 1997 National PTA celebrated its rich history of promoting the education, health, and safety of children and families for 100 years. A not-for-profit organization of parents, educators, students, and other citizens active in their schools and communities, the National PTA is a leader in reminding our nation of its obligations to children.

Building Successful Partnerships: A Guide for Developing Parent and Family Programs is based on the Mission and the Objects of the National PTA, and it is just one of many family and parent involvement initiatives undertaken by the organization.

THE MISSION OF THE NATIONAL PTA IS

- To support and speak on behalf of children and youth in the schools, in the community, and before governmental agencies and other organizations that make decisions affecting children

- To assist parents in developing the skills they need to raise and protect their children

- To encourage parent and public involvement in the public schools of this nation

THE OBJECTS OF THE NATIONAL PTA ARE

- To promote the welfare of children and youth in the home, school, community, and place of worship

- To raise the standards of home life

- To secure adequate laws for the care and protection of children and youth

- To bring into closer relation the home and the school so that parents and teachers may cooperate intelligently in the education of children and youth

- To develop between educators and the general public such united efforts as will secure for all children and youth the highest advantages in physical, mental, social, and spiritual education

In August 1999, National PTA launched a major initiative to train PTA leaders to present the organization's new Building Successful Partnerships program. Throughout the country, U.S. Virgin Islands, and in Department of Defense schools in Europe and the Pacific, PTA leaders are available to give presentations on the benefits of parent involvement, the components of effective parent involvement programs, and ways to implement the National Standards for Parent/Family Involvement Programs.

The National PTA has also become involved in creating federal legislation in the area of parent involvement. The Parental Accountability, Recruitment, and Education National Training Act (PARENT Act) was introduced in the House and the Senate in 1999. A National PTA-initiated bill, the PARENT Act was designed to help strengthen the involvement of parents in the education of their children by amending provisions within the Elementary and Secondary Education Act (ESEA). This would include expanding Title I's elementary and secondary programs' parent involvement requirements and ensuring that professional development activities for educators and school administrators include training on how to work with parents.

Membership in National PTA is open to anyone who is concerned with the education, health, and welfare of children and youth. PTA members have national representation before other education, health, and child advocacy organizations and on U.S. presidential-appointed committees. Members also have access to other national education organizations, technical assistance, training, resources/publications, National PTA's reference and research services, and National PTA's magazine, *Our Children*. For more information on National PTA membership, please call the Membership Department at (800) 307-4PTA (4782), or visit the National PTA's website at www.pta.org.

National PTA®

Headquarters:
330 North Wabash Avenue
Suite 2100
Chicago, Illinois 60611-3690
(312) 670-6782
(800) 307-4PTA (4782)
FAX: (312) 670-6783
e-mail: info@pta.org
website: www.pta.org

Washington, DC:
1090 Vermont Avenue
Washington, DC 20005-4905

About *Building Successful Partnerships* and the National Educational Service

The mission of the National Educational Service is to provide tested and proven resources that help those who work with youth create safe and caring schools, agencies, and communities where all children succeed. *Building Successful Partnerships* is just one of many resources and staff development opportunities NES provides that focus on building a community circle of caring. If you have any questions, comments, articles, manuscripts, or youth art you would like us to consider for publication, please contact us at the address below. Or visit our website at:

www.nesonline.com

Staff Development Opportunities Include:

Improving Schools through Quality Leadership
Integrating Technology Effectively
Creating Professional Learning Communities
Building Cultural Bridges
Discipline with Dignity
Ensuring Safe Schools
Managing Disruptive Behavior
Reclaiming Youth At Risk
Working with Today's Families

National Educational Service
1252 Loesch Road
Bloomington, IN 47404-9107
(812) 336-7700
(800) 733-6786 (toll-free number)
FAX (812) 336-7790
e-mail: nes@nesonline.com
www.nesonline.com

NEED MORE COPIES OR ADDITIONAL RESOURCES ON THIS TOPIC?

Need more copies of this book? Want your own copy? Need additional resources on this topic? If so, you can order additional materials by using this form or by calling us toll free at (800) 733-6786 or (812) 336-7700. Or you can order by FAX at (812) 336-7790, or visit our website at www.nesonline.com.

Title	Price*	Quantity	Total
Building Successful Partnerships	$ 18.95		
Parents Assuring Student Success	23.95		
How Smart Schools Get and Keep Community Support	24.95		
Professional Learning Communities at Work video	495.00		
Professional Learning Communities at Work book	24.95		
Creating the New American School	21.95		
The Principal as Staff Developer	21.95		
Beyond Piecemeal Improvements	23.95		
Creating Learning Communities	18.95		
Adventure Education for the Classroom Community	89.00		
		SUBTOTAL	
		SHIPPING	
Please add 5% of order total. For orders outside the continental U.S., please add 7% of order total.			
		HANDLING	
Please add $3. For orders outside the continental U.S., please add $5.			
		TOTAL (U.S. funds)	

*Price subject to change without notice.

❏ Check enclosed   ❏ Purchase order enclosed
❏ Money order   ❏ VISA, MasterCard, Discover, or American Express (circle one)

Credit Card No._____ Exp. Date_____
Cardholder Signature _____

SHIP TO:
First Name_____ Last Name_____
Position _____
Institution Name_____
Address_____
City_____ State_____ ZIP_____
Phone_____ FAX_____
E-mail _____

National Educational Service
1252 Loesch Road
Bloomington, IN 47404-9107
(812) 336-7700 • (800) 733-6786 (toll-free number)
FAX (812) 336-7790
e-mail: nes@nesonline.com • www.nesonline.com